THE
HIDDEN
ARMY

THE HIDDEN ARMY

MI9'S SECRET FORCE AND THE UNTOLD STORY OF D-DAY

**MATT RICHARDS &
MARK LANGTHORNE**

JOHN BLAKE

Published by John Blake Publishing,
an imprint of Kings Road Publishing
2.25, The Plaza,
535 Kings Road,
Chelsea Harbour
London, SW10 0SZ

www.johnblakebooks.com

www.facebook.com/johnblakebooks 🅵
twitter.com/jblakebooks 🆃

This edition published in 2018

Hardback ISBN: 978 1 78606 902 3
Trade Paperback ISBN: 978 1 78606 992 4

British Library Cataloguing-in-Publication Data:

A catalogue record for this book is available from the British Library.

Design by www.envydesign.co.uk

Printed and bound in Great Britain by Clays Ltd, Elcograf S.p.A.

1 3 5 7 9 10 8 6 4 2

Papers used ... ... products made from
wood grov ... ... sses conform to the
... ... igin.

Every attem ... ... it–holders, but some
were unobta ... ... ople could contact us.

... ... iblishing

*Dedicated to those who planned it, those who lived it,
and those who made it happen.*

CONTENTS

FOREWORD

For over ten years I have worked with Matt Richards on a number of documentaries he has directed on warfare within various conflicts of the twentieth century. These have included the stories of the International Brigaders from Britain who travelled to Spain to fight fascism in the Spanish Civil War, the British POWs who used every ounce of ingenuity to attempt to escape from Colditz Castle in World War II, and the extraordinary men who took part in the legendary Dambuster raid on German dams in 1943 using Barnes Wallis's fabled bouncing bombs.

In this book, Matt, along with his co-author Mark Langthorne, has uncovered and brought to life yet another compelling chapter in the history of World War II. It's a tale of determination, secrecy, and of courage. But unlike Colditz or the Dambusters, this story is hardly known and barely believable.

THE HIDDEN ARMY

Airey Neave and his plan for what became known as Operation Sherwood appears the stuff of fiction. After all, who would possibly propose hiding hundreds of Allied airmen and troops within yards of a major German stronghold in France in the run-up to D-Day? But this story is completely true, and all the more remarkable for it.

By expertly weaving together contemporary interviews, archive material and first-hand witness accounts within a dynamic narrative, Matt and Mark have created a fascinating and thrilling window into this vital operation.

Throughout this excellent book, we feel the dangers and risks to all those involved; from the French Resistance to the MI9 agents to the downed airmen and troops themselves in a time and place where the constant shadow of betrayal lurked heavily in their minds.

They reveal a mission that was almost foolhardy in its concept and one that divided opinions within MI9. And, above all, they adroitly portray the main characters involved in this striking story – ordinary men now suddenly undertaking extraordinary feats in the heat of warfare.

As well as being a welcome and worthy addition to the canon of historical literature about World War II, this book is also a timely reminder of the sacrifices made by ordinary men and women who showed a steely courage almost impossible to comprehend today.

The Hidden Army will ensure that their courage is never forgotten.

MAX ARTHUR, OBE
LONDON, 2018

CHAPTER 1

INTO FRANCE

'It's been described as a miracle. I think it probably was.'
RAY WORRALL, 44 SQN, BOMBER COMMAND

It was 25 July 1944 and twenty-year-old flight engineer Ray Worrall had less than a minute to live. Somewhere deep over enemy territory his Lancaster bomber was plummeting towards Earth, the ground below rushing up towards him at breakneck speed, the howl of the wind deafening.

Only a few hours earlier he had joined his crew in the mess at RAF Dunholme Lodge in Lincolnshire, had eaten egg and chips – a luxury in wartime Britain – then boarded Lancaster ME694. He clambered into his seat beside Flying Officer Dudley Ibbotson and made vital last-minute checks as night fell. It was Worrall's twenty-sixth mission over Germany, having volunteered to join the RAF in January 1943.

The mood in the aircraft as they prepared to take off was one of high stress and low morale. Each of those onboard knew that, with every mission, their odds of survival fell. Bomber Command crew members in World War II had a worse chance of survival than an infantry officer in World War I[1] and, statistically, there was little prospect of surviving a full tour of thirty operations, with only one in six expected to survive their first tour.[2]

With just a handful of missions left, Worrall's Lancaster thundered down the runway. Reaching 3,000 revs and full boost it crawled skywards, the weight of its fuel and bombs straining every ounce of thrust from the four Rolls-Royce engines. Climbing slowly, they headed north as they always did before banking over Lincoln Cathedral and making their way south towards Europe. 'You think you'll never see the UK again,' said Worrall. 'As we turned over the cathedral a lot of us used to look down and see it there, people wandering about on a summer's evening, and we were off to maybe get killed.'

Their target this July night was Stuttgart, an important industrial target in south-west Germany. The city was home to the Daimler and Porsche factories, had several military bases and was a railway hub. It was a crucial target and had already been bombed the night before with Worrall's Lancaster one of many planes dropping their bombs from 20,000 feet. But that raid had not been a success, most of the bombs fell short and the Lancasters faced fierce resistance from German night fighters based near the south of the city. The result was twenty-three Allied aircraft missing and the targets remained intact. Despite these losses, the squadron was ordered to return the following night.

Gaining height, Worrall's Lancaster was now turning towards the Channel and Caen in enemy territory. 'We used to make sure when we crossed the coast we were about 15,000 feet,' he recalled, adding 'anyone lagging behind would be picked off.'

As a flight engineer, Worrall's job largely consisted of monitoring the engines and fuel systems, leaving the pilot free to concentrate on his instruments and flying controls. Behind Worrall and the pilot – flying officer Ibbotson – the rest of the crew manned their positions: mid upper gunner Tom Whitehand, rear gunner Frank Wells, wireless operator Ken Andrews, navigator Ted Greatz and bomb aimer Ian Murray. Strangers before the war, they had been thrown together at random and now were more than colleagues and friends because their very lives depended on each other.

Reaching the required height the Lancasters flew gracefully over the Channel and headed towards Stuttgart. 'The Lancaster looked good from every angle, strongly shaped and well proportioned. In flight she appeared both powerful and balanced. Some aeroplanes seem to lean forward anxiously as they fly, others to be protestingly pushed along from behind, but the Lancaster rode the air easily and steadily,' remembered fellow pilot Jack Currie.[3]

Around Caen, the Lancasters encountered anti-aircraft flak and a number of aircraft were brought down. German fighters were also in the area causing havoc amongst the bombers. Worrall could only watch, in familiar horror, an exchange of tracer bullets flashing through the night sky as the German planes attacked one of the squadron. Moments later a Lancaster burst into flames and plummeted. Helpless, Worrall watched the aircraft as it dropped through the sky.

Managing to break through these initial defences, the remaining Lancasters pushed on deep into enemy territory. As they crossed France things quietened down somewhat, a brief respite for all the crews until they reached heavily defended Germany. But on this night Ray Worrall's Lancaster never reached its target.

Without warning, the crew suddenly felt a large thump smack the plane. It hit the rear and sent it into a steep dive. Ibbotson pulled desperately on the control column, but couldn't get the aircraft out of its furious dive. He called Worrall to help but they were rapidly losing height and the aircraft rattled and shook. It felt like it could disintegrate at any moment. The rest of the crew grabbed whatever they could to avoid being hurled forward as they struggled to put on their parachutes. Anything loose ricocheted throughout the inner fuselage. In the cockpit it became clear that the Lancaster was out of control. Ibbotson and Worrall could do nothing to stop it spinning to Earth. There was only one option. 'Bail out.'

Worrall put on his parachute and headed to the nose of the plane. Ian Murray had already opened the hatch and dived out along with half the crew. Worrall was next to jump but froze. If he didn't go immediately he'd be killed, with the remainder of the crew stuck behind him. But he didn't jump because he thought the order to bail out might have been rescinded, which he couldn't hear because he'd taken off his headset. 'On one occasion a pilot had given the order to bail out but then managed to get control of the aircraft and fly it back to base with half his crew, the other half having by then bailed out,' reflected Worrall. 'Was this to be my fate?'

Incapable of movement or clear thought, he was blocking the escape route. He pictured what would happen when the plane hit the ground; he thought about the heartbreak facing his parents, about not having enjoyed life more while he had had the chance. He prayed that the end would be quick. Then an urgent shout: 'Get a fucking move on!' It was Ted Greatz, the navigator. He was not ready to die. Worrall didn't have time to look round before Greatz kicked him hard in the kidneys and out the plane. Seconds later, Worrall's parachute opened with a reassuring jerk. As he descended, the black sky was suddenly lit by a massive explosion as his Lancaster crashed into the ground still fully laden with bombs. He didn't know it yet but all of his crew, bar one, had bailed out and survived. The only one not to make it was twenty-year-old Tom Whitehand.*

Worrall hit the ground heavily and found himself all alone in a field in France, bruised and shaken, but otherwise unharmed. He looked about, searching for his colleagues, but they were nowhere, having drifted off in other directions.

---

* There is some confusion over the name of Tom Whitehand. In Chorley Bomber Command losses he is named as Tom Whitehead. He is also down on 44 Sqn nom role as Tom Whitehead. However, in a letter dated 2 July 1969 to Tom Greatz, the Ministry of Defence clearly refer to him as T. W. Whitehand and confirm he was reported missing believed killed when Lancaster aircraft ME 694 was lost on the night of 25/26 July 1944. They state he was laid to rest in St. Pierre Cemetery, Plot No. 3, Row A, Grave No. 13.

Realising that German patrols would soon be on the scene, he knew there wasn't a moment to lose. After quickly burying his parachute he began moving as fast and as far away from the area as possible. This was the first time he had ever been on the ground outside Britain; he was alone, on the run with the enemy close by and didn't know which of the locals, if any, he could trust with his life.

He worked out that Caen was roughly two hundred and fifty miles to the north-west, and using his escape compass calculated which way to go and started walking through the night. When dawn broke, he took cover under a hedge and slept all morning. At sunset, he resumed his journey, keeping off the roads where possible as he knew there was a curfew and that anyone seen was liable to be shot. For the next two days and nights, Worrall followed this routine; sleeping by day under a hedge or in a haystack, travelling by night through fields and forests. It wasn't long before this tense nocturnal existence began to make him depressed and lonely. To make matters worse, he had barely eaten or had anything to drink since landing in France. His survival pack, containing chocolate, Horlicks tablets, water-purification tablets and energy pills, had almost run out and he had no idea about the fate of his crew. 'It is a rude awakening and a daunting experience to find yourself in a situation like this. You are all alone and everything you have taken for granted no longer exists. Your plight suddenly looms large,' he said.

While on the run, Worrall had two close calls. On one occasion he was approaching a village at dawn. In the centre was a crossroads and as he got closer he heard the unmistakable rumble of heavy vehicles. Close by was an open gate that led to a walled garden. He darted in and hid behind a bush. Moments later he watched as five German lorries, full of soldiers, passed by. And then a couple of days later he was walking down a narrow road that led to a T-junction. As he got closer he saw a German army car containing four soldiers approach the junction. There was nowhere to run, nowhere to hide.

He prayed that the vehicle would go straight over the junction, but the vehicle turned at right angles, heading straight for him. He was convinced his luck had run out. His rudimentary disguise of a brown linen jacket over his RAF battle dress and black flying boots hacked to bits with a penknife to resemble ordinary shoes would surely not fool even the most unobservant Nazi. So, with head bowed and collar turned up, he walked on. The car got closer and closer and Worrall expected imminent capture, his impending fate being either the rest of the war in a POW camp if he was lucky or execution if he wasn't. 'The car was travelling very slowly as it approached me,' he explained. 'But to my utter surprise and relief it passed me without stopping, so close I could have touched it, and continued on its way. I could not believe my luck.' When he summoned enough courage to look behind him, the vehicle had disappeared.

Worrall carried on, but it wasn't long before he almost gave himself away again. 'I was walking along a road and a young boy on a bicycle approached me and I was very foolish. I was chewing a piece of gum and that's what attracted his attention. I shouldn't have been doing that. No one chews gum in France. A silly thing to do. The boy asked me, "Are you RAF?", I said "Yes" and he said, "Follow me." He took me off the road and hid me under a hedge. "Lie down," he said, "and I'll go and get help."'

As he watched the boy disappear, Worrall knew he was in a vulnerable and dangerous position with no guarantees the boy wouldn't turn him in and return with Germans. But he was tired, hungry, fed up with sleeping rough and didn't feel he could go on much longer, so he decided to take a chance and put his faith in the boy.

'Then quite a big car came up and stopped beside me. The boy was in the passenger seat next to the driver. They both got out, shook hands and gave me a civilian overcoat to hide my crude disguise. I got in and we drove off,' Worrall added. They drove for some time before stopping and letting the boy out. The driver and Worrall continued, with the Englishman still worrying about his fate. Passing through the French countryside, the two men struck up a basic conversation. To Worrall's relief, the driver spoke good English. It turned out he was a doctor who had spent time in England in 1938 where he had married an English girl from Brighton who returned to France to live with him.

Late in the evening the car eventually arrived at a farmhouse where Worrall was warmly welcomed. He was given an omelette, water and shelter. Then they showed him a room with a double bed and two men asleep in it. He could scarcely believe his eyes: one of the men snoring heavily was the radio operator from his Lancaster, Ken

Andrews. Given a separate room, Worrall slept soundly until midday when he was woken by the farmer who told him that his pals were up – the second man in the bed was Ian Murray, his navigator – and that they could have free rein of the house during the day as long as they didn't go outside or near the windows as the neighbours would probably report anything strange.

The following morning, as they all went into the kitchen for breakfast, the downed airmen were greeted by two unfamiliar figures in civilian clothes. At first they thought they were locals but then they got nervous. Had they been betrayed?

The three were given threadbare and ill-fitting clothes by the two men and told they would be going on a long walk. Their destination was not revealed. Suspicions grew and tensions rose, but then the two explained. They were both RAF. One, Pete Berry, was English. The other, Pierre, a Belgian fighter pilot who'd joined the RAF after Dunkirk and been shot down some weeks earlier. They explained that they were going to take them to a place of safety; a hiding place so bold that it remains barely believable. A sanctuary right under the nose of the Nazis. It was part of an audacious plan devised by an ingenious army officer who was working in the shadows of a secret British service.

CHAPTER 2

ON THE RUN

R ay Worrall wasn't alone in being on the run in Europe in 1944. Scattered throughout the continent were other Allied airmen who had been shot down, and soldiers from North America and all four corners of the Commonwealth. During World War II about a quarter of a million Allied airmen and soldiers were stranded behind enemy lines, most incarcerated in prisoner of war camps. It is estimated that of this number, 3,000 to 5,000 evaded capture or escaped and made it back to Britain.[4] But, as Richard Garratt wrote, 'Every escaper is at heart an evader; whether every evader is an escaper seems less certain.'[5] He contends that when cast adrift in a hostile environment it is the nature of man to seek cover while also instinctively trying to make for home, a place synonymous with safety.

However, not all evaders did this. Some found themselves in rural communities untouched by the conflict, and decided they'd be better off seeing out the war undetected and living the life of a local rather than risking a perilous journey home. Even after the war they stayed in these communities, not so much because they felt at home there but because they faced charges of desertion should they reappear in Britain.

Like Worrall, Sergeant Cliff Hallett, a twenty-one-year-old mid upper gunner, was trapped behind enemy lines and he wasn't contemplating desertion either. He was desperate to get back to Britain. He found himself alone in France after his Halifax had been shot down by two German fighters. Separated from the rest of his crew – two had been killed and three had been rescued and taken away to a brothel in Paris – he had parachuted down to land on the airfield at St Andre. Hearing indistinct voices he ran away, fearing they might be Germans. Through the night, in pouring rain, Hallett crawled on all fours through fields of wheat until, feeling safe, he rested in the darkness. He was woken the following morning by voices. But they weren't English or French voices. They were German. Raising his head carefully he saw a sign saying '*Zutritt Verboten*' and realised he was on the edge of an enemy camp – and, even worse, still wearing his RAF uniform. Creeping away, Hallett was eventually taken in by a local farmer, who was a member of the Resistance, and given coffee, bread and a bed.

Soon Michel, another farmer and the head of the Resistance in the area, arrived. He interrogated Hallett, ensuring he was who he claimed to be, and then, satisfied with his answers and happy he wasn't a German infiltrator, gave him farm clothing, burnt his RAF uniform and took him to a safe-house in Nonancourt where he stayed for three weeks. (Hallett soon discovered that Michel had been arrested and executed for his Resistance activities just a week after he had interrogated him.)

Captain William H. Davis, an American pilot of 485 Fighter Squadron, was another behind enemy lines, one of the many Americans and Canadians downed over France. He explained:

I was shot down on 7 July 1944 while on a mission to bomb targets in the Loire region. We had buzzed four trains already and were about 20 miles north-west of Orleans when a lot of flak came up from a fifth train I was attacking. My right engine was shot away and the 'ship' began to burn. I came down in a ploughed field and, by luck, was only slightly hurt although it was a rough landing. I took off for some woods as soon as I could get rid of my 'chute. There were some farmers at the side of he field, gesticulating and coming towards me, but I remembered having been briefed not to ask help from a group of Frenchmen, so I decided to get away.

After I had been hiding in the woods for about an hour and had buried my flying suit and gloves, a young Frenchman found me. I told him I wanted civilian clothes and he went off, promising to return with them in half an hour. After one-and-a-half hours he had not come back so I left. I found another hiding place in the woods a mile away and stayed there all that night. Early next morning I started off again, walking west. I contacted a farmer and got some food at his house. He gave me civilian clothes and offered to take me to the Resistance. The local 'chief' took care of me for the next four days. I was moved every day, staying in a barn or field where Resistance members would bring me food. The Frenchmen told me they had sent a message to London and that I had been identified as a result.

Twenty-year-old air gunner Charlie 'Jock' Weir from Midlothian had also been shot down, early in the morning of 1 May 1944, when his Stirling was hit when attacked by a Ju 88. With his aircraft crippled by flames and four of his crew dead, Weir bailed out at 11,000 feet and found himself coming down near Fougenies in the middle of the French countryside.

The following morning seventeen-year-old René Capron travelled to the site of the plane crash on his motorbike to inspect the wreckage and to see if there were any survivors who his family could help but, before long, the Germans turned up and Capron had to flee. Returning later, he found Weir hiding and took him back to his family who sheltered him at their farm. However, after Weir had been interrogated by the head of the household, they thought he was a German pretending to be in the RAF. Protesting his innocence, Weir broke out into a fit of four-letter English words. 'My interrogators burst out laughing and said they had been fooled by my guttural Scottish accent. One said no German could use English like that,' Weir remembered. He was given a gamekeeper's jacket, trousers and wellington boots that were two sizes too small. Within weeks his feet were bleeding but he was safe. For the time, at least.

Meanwhile, Hayward Spinks, of USAAF 357 Fighter Group, had been shot down while on a strafing mission in north-west France and crash-landed near Eve. 'About ten Frenchmen gathered immediately and took me to a farmhouse where I was given farmer's clothing. I was taken from here to another farm, further from town, owned by a Polish family consisting of the farmer, his wife, two sons and daughter. They had lived in France since the last war,' he recalled. The Polish family took good care of Spinks and, using his underground contacts, the farmer managed to get Spinks to Paris along with three other airmen. There, they were taken to their hiding place in the Place d'Italie by a guide named Mlle Deplanche.

'In Paris I encountered probably my most unforgettable character during the war, Mme Yvonne Diximier. She was a widow in her late-forties who seemed to delight in showing her disdain for the Germans. In the three or four days that I stayed with her we toured Paris very much as a visitor would today, and she refused to pass a sidewalk café where there were Germans seated without our having a drink at a nearby table.' From Paris, Spinks was taken to Senlis where he stayed for another five weeks before being conveyed with a downed fighter pilot to Chantilly, where they stayed with a hairdresser who had radio contact with

England and passed on information about the progress of the war. Spinks and the fighter pilot waited here for three days while the Resistance planned their next move.

But the evaders weren't limited to downed aircrew. Twenty-six-year-old First Lieutenant William T. Dillon was platoon leader in the 16th Infantry Regiment of the US Army. On 5 July 1944 he was with a patrol that was suddenly cut off. During a brief engagement with the enemy, Dillon received shrapnel wounds in the arm and neck and was captured, along with the rest of his patrol, by the Germans. Without receiving any medical treatment for his wounds, Dillon was taken for interrogation before being moved to La Chapelle sur Vire then, finally, to a local hospital. 'Here they dressed my wounds and took pictures of us and drew silhouettes. The guards took all my personal property including my watch. I never saw it again,' Dillon said.

After three days at the hospital Dillon was taken, with others, to another camp where they rested briefly before beginning an escorted march towards yet another camp. On the first night of this march four Americans escaped. Dillon's mind was made up: he wasn't in the war to be a prisoner. 'The next night I escaped by jumping over a hedge. I hid in the middle of a field on the other side while the Germans looked for me for about an hour. The next day I contacted some locals who gave me clothes. They said that Spain was out of the question, so I decided to go to Switzerland,' he recalled. But Dillon never got to Switzerland. He met some Resistance fighters who helped him reunite with three of his platoon in Mortagne. The Resistance suggested they go down the Loire by boat and then escape by sea, but Dillon and his colleagues decided to take their chance by walking through France. Constantly evading Germans, they soon found themselves in the middle of France, deep behind enemy lines and in dire need of somewhere to hide, and someone to help them do so, until the advancing Allies could reach them after D-Day.

All these men – Worrall, Hallett, Davis, Weir, Spinks and Dillon – were hundreds of miles from home and safety. They were alone, on the run and being hunted. They had been told by intelligence officers that the Germans would only conduct an intensive search of the immediate area in which a downed Allied airman had been thought to land for a maximum of forty-eight hours. After that they'd give up. But these Allied airmen and soldiers were not highly trained members of the Special Forces who today are taught how to survive behind enemy lines, how to evade the enemy, how to cover their tracks and how to kill with bare hands. They hadn't been trained in the modern method of 'stress inoculation' when Special Forces soldiers are exposed to heartbeat-racing drills that raise their threshold for staying calm. 'It doesn't mean Special Forces soldiers are immune to stress or the mistakes that stress causes, but it takes a lot more to rattle one of them than an old-time draftee.'[6]

Remember, these Allied evaders were simply young men who only a few months previously had been living at home and had wives, girlfriends and family. Now their nearest and dearest would be receiving the dreaded telegram informing them of the plight of their husband, brother or son. On 29 July in Victoria, Australia, Ida Murray, the mother of Ian Murray, opened a telegram which informed her: 'Regret to inform you that your son is missing as a result air-operations on 26 July. Known details are he was a member of crew Lancaster aircraft detailed to attack enemy target at Stuttgart Germany which failed to return to base presumably due to enemy action. The Minister for Air joins with Air Board in expressing sincere sympathy in your anxiety.'

For the relatives, their lives were in turmoil. Such telegrams gave them no closure, the fate of those closest to them was still unknown. Likewise, the airmen now on the run in France had seen their world turned upside down. Before the war these men had jobs and were simply going about their daily lives. Now they had been involved in ferocious combat, had seen friends and colleagues killed before their eyes and were stuck behind enemy lines, totally dependent on their ability to make the right decision and on people they desperately hoped they could trust. They had to adapt and cope quickly, sizing up their situation and developing their own strategy to survive in a new and threatening environment. Essentially, things boiled down to 'the will to survive', the determination to live regardless of an extreme situation.

All they had to rely on was what little evasion training they'd had and a small escape kit. For example, American airmen were given a red purse that contained maps of France, Holland, Belgium, Germany, Spain and Portugal as well as 2,000 French francs, worth roughly $50 – a significant amount given that the average monthly rent at the time was $40. They also carried three or four passport photos to be used by the Resistance to create forged documents, chocolate, a tube of milk, Benzedrine tablets to counter fatigue, Halazone tablets to purify water, matches, chewing gum, a compass and Horlicks tablets.

But whatever kit they carried and whatever basic training they'd had, they were now disoriented in a strange environment and isolated, often suffering from increasing depression, cognitive impairment, sleep disturbance, loss of appetite, fear and anxiety. Combined, these would have a detrimental effect on the evaders' ability to make the right choices and, consequently, survive long enough to make it home. And make it home was their plan. Their duty was not to stay and fight but to escape back to Britain as soon as possible because the aviators in particular, who had taken two years to train and get battle ready, were desperately needed back in the air again. But escaping was a massive undertaking, being completely dependent on strangers (and even children) who shuttled them between safe houses under cover of darkness. The threat of betrayal never went away. And their situation was even more complicated because the railway lines and the communication infrastructure that they relied on had been incapacitated by intensive Allied bombing in the period prior to the D–Day invasion.

Getting these men back would be easier said than done. The authorities, intelligence agencies and secret forces would be required to oversee an escape and evasion programme the likes of which had never been seen before.

THE HIDDEN ARMY

But get them back they must, especially the airmen who couldn't easily be replaced and who were vital if the Allies were going to win the war.

CHAPTER 3

OVER THERE

For downed airmen, such as Worrall, hiding in France, Belgium, Holland, etc., the urge to get back to Britain was based on freedom, self-preservation, a desire to be reunited with loved ones and, more often than not, desperation to get back into action. For the RAF however, their main concern was simply getting airmen back so that they could resume their duties and continue to make a valuable contribution to the war effort. Time and money had been invested in their intensive, highly specialised training and, while aircraft could be built quickly (in the summer of 1943 a stunt between the Ministry of War and the RAF saw an operational Wellington bomber built from scratch, at the Broughton factory in North Wales, in a record time of 23 hours and 50 minutes*), training aircrew was a much

---

* At its peak, the factory employed 6,000 people, more than half being women, to work 12-hour shifts in order to churn out 28 Wellington bombers a week.

lengthier process. And getting back these downed airmen also reduced the need to train replacements, especially given the rapid technical advances in aviation that were taking place in the 1940s. No matter how long they had been on the run, they 'could be fed with little trouble onto existing courses, before going back onto operations'.[7]

Returning evaders and escapers also provided an incredible boost to their nearest and dearest, colleagues in their squadrons and the wider community who were all suffering the hardships of war. They illustrated that escape was possible, that all was not lost if a pilot had to bail out over Europe and that, despite overwhelming odds, they *could* make their way back to Britain. It was a triumph of sorts and in the dark days of war any victory, however small, had a significant boost to national morale. 'The miracle of their reappearance at Air Force bases and stations had a marvellous effect, as I was able to witness, on the morale of all who flew against Germany,' wrote Airey Neave.[8]

Additionally, any escaper or evader might return with vital intelligence and information about the enemy. Extensive debriefing sessions prised this information from them and helped the British secret service build up a better picture of many aspects of the enemies' operations, plans and military might. Furthermore, the escapers and evaders were a frustrating, time-consuming distraction for the enemy, pulling them away from other duties and the battlefield, tying them up in non-operational searches.

The emphasis placed upon the repatriation of downed airmen by the British (and later the US) authorities also highlights how much air warfare had changed in the years between World Wars I and II. During the 1914–18 conflict, aircraft were nothing more than flimsy materials somehow bound together and built only to fight. By 1939, aircraft had advanced technically and aerodynamically. The likes of the iconic Spitfire were now built to win. As Robert Fisk wrote: 'The Spitfire was to previous aircraft design as Auden was to Robert Graves. In art, the Spitfire was Vorticism against the Romantics – sleek, new, frightening, unforgiving.'[9]

Aircraft provided Britain with its first decisive victory of World War II during the Battle of Britain, but it was a battle in which the Spitfire only had a supporting part. Despite all the romanticism surrounding the plane – its name being synonymous with victory in the air – it has now become accepted that without the Hawker Hurricane, designed by Sir Sydney Camm, the Battle of Britain could never have been won. When the Battle of Britain began in July 1940, Fighter Command consisted of 29 Hurricane squadrons and 19 Spitfire squadrons. The Spitfire was constructed of metal and simply couldn't be manufactured as quickly as the Hurricane, whose fuselage was constructed partly of wood and fabric, which meant that any damaged planes were reasonably straightforward to repair.

The first Hurricanes went into service with 111 Squadron in December 1937. In April that same year the Luftwaffe, in conjunction with the Italian Condor Legion, had used aerial power to launch a devastating bombing raid on the Basque town of Guernica during which 170–300 civilians were killed.[10] This raid is widely recognised as being the first intentional targeting of civilians by aerial bombers[11], although Mussolini had made use of air power to attack Abyssinian positions at Walwal in December 1934 and, even earlier, during World War I, Germany had used Zeppelins to bomb British towns and cities causing 1,400 deaths.

The interwar years, as illustrated by the Condor Legion's raid on Guernica, had focused on aerial tactics and strategic bombardment to defeat an enemy. Giulio Douhet encapsulated the claims for strategic air power by suggesting that 'striking directly at civilian centres with bombs or chemicals would bring states to their knees because civilians could not withstand such pounding.'[12] By the outbreak of World War II, air warfare had changed dramatically and pilots had not only become a valuable commodity but iconic figures, heroes, similar to an 'ancient warrior ... now mounted in a lethal machine that elevated him above all earthly mortals, ready for repeated trials by combat on behalf of the honour and survival of his nation.'[13]

The RAF had used the interwar years to try to devise a plan that utilised air power to offer an effective form of defence against an attack on Britain while also believing that the best form of defence was actually to attack, either as a deterrent or taking the battle to the heart of the enemy. The Battle of Britain, thanks to the Hurricane, had seen the defence element of these tactics bear fruit, seemingly against the odds. 'It was the aircraft for the right season,' said renowned test pilot Eric 'Winkles' Brown. 'It came at a time when it literally saved the country and it performed magnificently.'[14]

In September 1940, referring to the policy of attack, Winston Churchill wrote, 'the bombers alone will provide the means for victory' and he poured vast resources into Bomber Command to take the fight to the heart of German towns and cities. Right up until September 1945, Bomber Command would launch a staggering 389,000 sorties on the Nazi regime and its supporters. With targets protected by anti-aircraft defences and squadrons of Messerschmitt fighters, each mission was terrifying. Over 8,000 bombers were shot down or crash-landed during these sorties; in one single night 670 men of Bomber Command were killed in a matter of hours when they were ambushed by the Luftwaffe on their way to Nuremberg. 'There was an aching silence in the mess that night,' one pilot recalled. 'We had lost so many good chaps, the cream of our youth.'[15] Of 125,000 aircrew who served in Bomber Command, almost 57,000 were killed and another 18,000 wounded or taken prisoner, a staggering casualty rate of 60 per cent.[16]

Every aircraft lost or damaged could be replaced or repaired, taking only weeks at most. But the training of pilots and aircrews simply couldn't keep up because that would take years. As the war progressed and ever more bombing raids took place over Europe, the number of airmen being shot down increased with the knock-on effect being a severe shortage of trained airmen in Britain. It was vital to get any downed pilots and aircrew back on active service as quickly as possible, no mean feat considering many had been taken prisoner of war while others were on the run or in hiding.

Fortunately, even before the war had begun, British agencies had started wondering how Allied servicemen might escape or evade capture on the Continent and how they might be repatriated to Britain. As the dark shadow of conflict began to creep across Europe, and with war seemingly imminent, urgent attention began to be paid to the possible creation of an organisation that would cater for the needs of both escapers and evaders.

Towards the end of World War I, a small intelligence directorate named MI1a had been formed following the realisation amongst military intelligence that escapers and evaders might well provide a valuable source of untapped intelligence material. In 1938, Captain A.R. Rawlinson and Major J.C.F. Holland concluded that something similar might be required given developments in Europe, and in October 1939 they submitted a detailed paper outlining the organisation that might be required. As a result, on 23 December 1939 a new intelligence section was formed with a specific remit focusing on escape and evasion.

Its name was MI9 and it started life in a London hotel bedroom.

CHAPTER 4

THE TOBACCONIST

The moment Flight Lieutenant Berry hit the ground he was knocked out cold. It was 2.30 am and he had landed in a field in France in the dead of night. Regaining consciousness he saw he was missing his right boot and blood was oozing from superficial wounds to his lip and eyebrow. There was no one around and it was deathly silent. Nearby he spotted a thicket, and gathering up his parachute he stumbled towards it. As quietly as he could, he buried it in one location then moved to another part of the thicket to bury his harness and Mae West lifejacket. Then he sat back against a tree and tried to make sense of his situation.

Prior to the outbreak of war, Leslie Frederick Berry had been a wholesale tobacconist in central London. It was a boom time for him because cigarette smoking had increased dramatically ever since tobacco companies had provided soldiers fighting overseas in World War I with free cigarettes every day, claiming they were doing their part to 'help' our boys. In 1915 alone, British soldiers and sailors smoked 1,000 tons of cigarettes and 700 tons of pipe tobacco. The previous year the trade journal *Tobacco* had claimed in its editorial that 'it might also be said that a man in the firing line first thinks of his cartridges and the very next thing he seems to worry about is ammunition for his pipe. The pipe itself is only less precious than the rifle.'[17] In addition, smoking had become associated with sophisticated femininity during the interwar years, embodying in women new ideals and opportunities.

Conversely, in Nazi Germany, by the outbreak of World War II smoking was discouraged in the workplace and banned in cinemas and schools. Policemen and servicemen were not permitted to smoke in public in uniform. Moreover, cigarette advertising was restricted and women were not allowed to buy cigarettes in cafés and other public places. 'Nazi officials moved aggressively in an all-out campaign against cigarette smoking in which tobacco was proclaimed "an enemy of the people".'[18] Hitler was always keen to point out that he had quit smoking in 1919, and that fellow fascists Mussolini and Franco were also non-smokers, unlike Allied leaders Churchill, Stalin and Roosevelt.

Naturally, the Nazi attitude to smoking didn't concern Berry but their march across Europe did, and on the outbreak of war he joined the RAF. He was thirty-one years old when he joined up, considerably older than many other conscripts, most of whom were in their early twenties or even younger. His relative maturity and experience was a big help when, later in the war, he found himself in the camp at Forêt de Fréteval.

By May 1944, Berry was a flight lieutenant serving as a rear gunner on Lancaster bombers. Just before midnight on 31 May he took off from RAF Mildenhall in Suffolk on a bombing run to the marshalling yards at Trappes, in the western suburbs of Paris.

The flight across the English Channel had been routine but above the French coast the flak became thick, intense and frightening as the German anti-aircraft defence homed in on their targets. Each burst made it seem likely that it was inevitable they would be hit. The seven-man crew could smell and taste the cordite from the explosions through their oxygen masks, the black of night briefly illuminated by the swirling white shafts of searchlights and the orange flashes of flak.

Passing through the anti-aircraft fire without incident, the captain radioed back to confirm all his crew were okay. They were unharmed, although shaken. The plane pressed on to its target.

After midnight, the chill of the air at 7,000 feet began to bite, especially in the rear turret where Berry sat strapped in: cold, alone and vulnerable. His was the most dangerous position in the plane. Rear gunners were known as 'Tail End Charlies' and their life expectancy was minimal, most estimates suggesting just five sorties. His small turret was designed for functionality not comfort and was very cold because the Perspex had been cut away from the front to give better vision. Frostbite was a real possibility, and that's why rear gunners would often spread anti-freeze on their faces before take off.

At about 2 am Berry saw the sight every rear gunner and all Lancaster crews feared: the onrushing shape of German night-fighters, barely visible in the dark but still unmistakable. He reported it immediately and prepared for action as the Lancaster lurched to try to avoid attack. With a fighter 500 yards away and closing, Berry gave it a short burst of gunfire, his .303 calibre weapons nothing more than pop guns compared to the lethal canon on a Junkers (Ju) 88. It flashed past them, Berry unable to follow its trajectory from his rear-gun turret. 'I told the pilot to corkscrew to starboard. The Ju passed underneath and appeared on our port beam up, flew level for a minute, attacked and passed underneath and appeared on our starboard beam up,' Berry said. Then it came in to attack again. 'In spite of our evasive action,' he added, 'I could not get the rear guns to bear on him and could not touch him. This was my fifth combat, and the pilot was clever and knew his job.'

When the mid-upper gunner failed to fire on the German, Berry assumed, correctly, that he must have been killed in the attack. As he waited for the fighter to come around again he realised that the Lancaster was on fire. 'Sheets of flame went by the rear turret and I saw the Ju starboard beam up, coming again in our direction,' he said. Like Worrall and countless other airmen during World War II, Berry's life expectancy suddenly snapped short. It could be only a matter of minutes, seconds even, before the Ju's bullets ripped through the flimsy fuselage of the Lancaster. Over the intercom, Berry heard a command from the cockpit: 'The captain ordered us to bail out. I centralised the turret and opened the doors and entered the fuselage.' The sight that greeted him in the cramped space was terrifying. The aircraft was furiously ablaze and there was no sign of any of his colleagues in the fierce heat. Berry looked around briefly, called out, but there was no response. Then he did the only thing he could; he grabbed his parachute and bailed out by the entrance door. 'The aircraft went down in a screaming dive, on fire from nose to stern. We were flying at 7,000 feet when first attacked and, having no idea how far we had dropped, I pulled the ripcord immediately. The parachute, in opening, knocked me out for a bit and cut my lip and eyebrow. The next thing I knew I was in the air, saw my parachute above me and knew I was alive. Then I saw the aircraft blazing on the ground about ten miles north. I looked around for other parachutes but could not see any.'

As he floated down, Berry tried to get his bearings. To the south-east he was sure he could make out the searchlights and anti-aircraft guns of Paris and below him a long road, two woods and a large, isolated château. He decided that he would make for the château on landing.

He hit the ground. Hard.

He was briefly knocked out, and then hid his parachute and other equipment in the nearby thicket. Certain there was nobody around he warily crossed some fields and cautiously approached the building. It was shuttered and silent. Seeing cows nearby, Berry was convinced that somebody must be living there. Picking up a handful of stones, he tossed them up at the shutters, but no response. Then he wandered up a lane by the side of the house and looked around; there wasn't another house for miles. He opened his escape kit, took out the money and checked his bearings. He wondered what to do; how to survive.

He decided his only option was to return to the château. He opened a creaking door at the back of the property and went up some stone steps to another door that was locked. Rattling to try and open it, Berry finally roused one of the occupants. High above, a window opened up and an elderly man leaned out, peering into the darkness before shouting out in French. Unable to speak the language fluently, Berry responded in English, telling the old man that he was an English airman. '*Allez, allez, promenade,*' replied the Frenchman. In desperation Berry threw his wallet up to him because it contained English money, hoping he'd understand. Catching the wallet, the old man inspected it and then disappeared from view. Berry heard some shouting, then silence.

He waited, wondering what was happening. Finally, he heard the door locks rattle and open, and there stood the old man's two sons, scared and worried. Berry immediately offered them some Player's cigarettes, which calmed them down, and they beckoned him to follow into a barn. Bizarrely, no sooner had Berry entered the barn than he found himself helping them to deliver a foal. After more reassurances that he was a '*parachutiste*' they led him back to the château, gave him two eggs to eat and then took him to a small cottage in the grounds where he slept for the rest of the night.

The next morning Berry was woken by the two Frenchmen and a third man, bursting in with some breakfast. The latter demanded to see Berry's escape photographs and took two from him before leaving without uttering another word. Later that afternoon he returned, and Berry discovered why he had taken the two photos when he handed him a freshly forged identity card. As Berry changed into the civilian clothes that the Frenchman had brought him, he was told to act deaf and dumb when out and about. And with that, the Frenchman disappeared.

Berry was unsure what to do. Unable to converse with the old man or his sons he decided he should simply wait in the cottage and see what happened. He knew they wouldn't turn him in and the identity card meant that the Resistance was working away in the background. Surely somebody or something would turn up soon. And it did – later that afternoon another Frenchman arrived, a lawyer who could speak good English. He whisked Berry away in his black Citroën, but not before Berry handed over the last English money he had – £6, 10s – to the elderly man and his sons. The lawyer told Berry that he was the only one to escape from the burning Lancaster and that his crewmates had already been given a proper burial. Berry was all too aware of the risks faced by Lancaster crews. He knew that every mission could be their last. Nevertheless, the loss of his friends hit him hard. He had to make it home, for himself and for their memory.

The lawyer took Berry to the home of a man who taught English in the local school, and he stayed for two nights. Returning with a new suit and shoes, the lawyer then drove Berry to Clermont where he was joined by two more downed airmen, Flight Sergeant Pepall, like Berry a rear gunner in the RAF, whose Short Stirling bomber* had been shot down during an attack on a railway depot on 20 April, and a Canadian navigator, William ('Bill') Brayley, who had been shot down on 11 April and was only one of three survivors from his aircraft. They were driven to the railway station in Chantilly where they were given a ticket each and, with a young female guide, were put on a train for Paris, 20 miles away. In Paris their guide ushered them onto a metro train that was full of German soldiers. The journey shouldn't have taken long but, according to Berry, the train had to stop for an hour when the air raid sirens began wailing, 'during which we stood for an hour between SS troops and pretended to be half asleep.'

Finally, the train was given the all clear and reached its destination where, undiscovered, Berry, Brayley and Pepall were led by their guide to a bicycle shop where they were greeted by another woman, Anne, who took them to the flat of Philippe d'Albert Lake, the head of the Paris Resistance. Here they met Philippe's American wife, Virginia, and

---

* Stirlings were designed by the Short Brothers firm and were the first four-engine heavy bombers used by Britain in the war, entering service in 1941. Despite being one of the most important RAF planes of World War II, its role has largely been forgotten by history, possibly because they were unable to carry a maximum load of bombs farther than 590 miles.

were given a severe interrogation to confirm their identity before meeting two other evaders, the American airmen Thomas Yankus and Jim Pearson III.

On meeting the Lakes, Berry was excited by the work being done by the French Resistance and suggested he join them. Even Pepall wanted in, but Philippe was quick to subdue their eagerness; 'Philippe said I should get plenty of excitement before long,' Berry noted, unaware at the time that plans were being made for a bold and ambitious evasion plan that would see the Allies attempt to deceive the Germans with the help of the Resistance thanks to a simple but audacious scheme.

And Flight Lieutenant Leslie Frederick Berry would be an integral – yet ultimately divisive – figure within this plan, one that had been hatched by MI9 in a London hotel bedroom.

CHAPTER 5

THE AGENCY

The Metropole Hotel opened in 1885 on Northumberland Avenue, the second hotel on that road to be constructed by the Gordon Hotels Company. Its original 88-page brochure advertised it as a hotel particularly suited to women and families visiting the West End, travellers from Paris and the Continent arriving at Charing Cross from Dover and Folkestone, officers attending the levées (ie. royal receptions) at St James's Palace, ladies going to the drawing rooms, state balls and concerts at Buckingham Palace, and colonial and American visitors unused to the great world of London. Prosperous at the turn of the century, it became a popular venue for banquets, balls and dinner parties. The Prince of Wales (later King Edward VII) is even rumoured to have entertained guests there.

At the outbreak of World War I the hotel was requisitioned to provide accommodation for government staff, and Winston Churchill was stationed there when he was Minister of Munitions from 1917 to 1919. As Big Ben chimed the end of The Great War, Churchill looked out of his window at the eleventh hour of the eleventh day of the eleventh month as everyone poured into the streets to celebrate. He wondered whether this really was the war to end all wars or it was it merely another chapter in a 'cruel and senseless story? Will a new generation in their turn be immolated to square the black accounts of Teuton and Gaul?'

After the war, the Metropole reopened as a hotel until 1936 when it was leased to the government for £300,000. It now provided alternative accommodation for the various departments that had been removed from Whitehall Gardens to make way for the construction of the new block of government offices.

Towards the end of the decade, with the prospect of war becoming ever more likely, the country began bracing itself for the worst as the tide of fascism spread across Europe. In March 1938, German troops marched into Austria and six months later the Sudetenland region of Czechoslovakia was handed over to Germany following meetings between Hitler and the British prime minster, Neville Chamberlain, which resulted in The Munich Agreement. This stated that Hitler could have the Sudetenland on the basis that he promised not to invade the rest of Czechoslovakia. But in March 1939 Germany did just that. Believing Poland would be the next target for Hitler, Britain and France threatened military action. Chamberlain believed that faced with the prospect of war against Britain and France, Hitler would step back but he was wrong again; on 1 September 1939 Germany invaded Poland. Two days later, Chamberlain broadcast to the nation that Britain was at war with Germany.

Almost immediately it was recognised that Britain would need a specialist organisation to support the activities of potential POWs and to establish guidelines for escape and evasion across Europe. In November and December 1939, GHQ British Expeditionary Force recommended to the Director of Military Intelligence that such an organisation should be set up in the War Office specifically to facilitate escapes of British prisoners from enemy prison camps.* The matter was considered by Military Intelligence Research, who advised agreement. As a result, on 23 December 1939, MI9 was created and their first office was a room, Number 424, at the Metropole Hotel. 'MI9's original, vast single room in the Metropole Hotel was hardly suitable for the sort of business its staff had to transact, and they had to work in it long before the open-plan office became fashionable. At least they worked fast, in the breathing-space afforded by the lull in actual fighting.'[19]

The objectives of MI9 were:

- To facilitate escapes of British POWs, thereby getting back service personnel and containing additional enemy manpower on guard duties.

---

* Two months earlier a World War I escaper, M.C.C. Harrison, sent the Director of Military Intelligence a long and convincing letter advocating an inter-service department that would help POWs to escape. In the letter he argued the need for suitable compasses, maps and money as part of a basic escape kit. This document was passed on to J.C.F. Holland.

- To facilitate the return to the United Kingdom of those who succeeded in evading capture in enemy occupied territory.

- To collect and distribute information.

- To assist in the denial of information to the enemy.

- To maintain morale of British POWs in enemy prison camps.

The whole subject of POWs had changed significantly, especially during World War I. Previously, the idea of being captured and held prisoner had carried with it a shameful, ignominious stigma. But slowly, as The Great War progressed, the value of escaping prisoners returning to reveal vital intelligence was recognised, as was the boost such escapes gave to the morale of the nation, the Services and the families of those concerned. In addition, such escapes led to the enemy's resources being significantly diverted from front-line action. Consequently, even before the outbreak of World War II, ex-POW escapers from the 1914–18 conflict were asked to provide MI1[*] with essential advice.[20]

---

[*] MI1 was a sub-branch of Military Intelligence established in 1917 and concerned mainly with the interrogation of German POWs once they reached the UK. These men had already been questioned in France following their capture, but it was thought that further questioning in the UK might reveal more gems of intelligence, particularly those of a specialised nature. At the same time, MI1 considered that British officers held in German prisoner of war camps might also have useful observations or fragments of overheard conversation that might provide significant intelligence, and so they devised a code by which a seemingly innocent letter could convey top secret messages.

THE AGENCY

The man placed in charge of MI9 upon its formation was Major Norman Crockatt DSO, MC, a soldier who had served during World War I, was wounded twice during the retreat from Mons, had been awarded the Military Cross in 1917 and was mentioned in despatches during the Palestine conflict. Born in 1894, he had retired from the army in 1927 to work in the London Stock Exchange but was lured out of retirement to head up the new intelligence service by an old school chum, J.C.F. Holland, who himself had won the DFC as a pilot, worked with Lawrence of Arabia and had fought in the Irish Troubles.

Holland had rejected the suggestion that the role should be filled by someone who had experience of a successful escape in World War I and instead chose Crockatt, a formidable, quick-witted man who wasn't restricted by red tape. Moreover, he attracted loyalty and devotion from all who served under him and was described by M.R.D. Foot and J.M. Langley as a man with a 'natural grace of bearing, set off by a tall well-proportioned figure and piercing greenish eyes, [which] made him a noticeable man in any company: in an age of drab clothes and battledress he wore at every opportunity the colourful gear of his regiment, the Royal Scots.'[21]

But whilst Crockatt had served with distinction as a soldier he had never been captured and, consequently, lacked any experience of being a prisoner of the enemy. To counter this, Crockatt decided that the knowledge of former POWs, especially those who had successfully escaped, should be exploited and he set about appointing them as lecturers at

MI9's training school to teach service personnel how to behave in the event of capture, with the emphasis on the duty *not* to be taken prisoner and to escape if captured.[22]

Just a few months after it had been formed, MI9 faced a crisis of potentially catastrophic proportions when the British Expeditionary Force (BEF) found itself at Dunkirk awaiting evacuation as German forces bore down on them. Over 300,000 men were on the beaches yet few, if any, had been schooled in escape and evasion work. Despite the best efforts of the 'little ships' during the heroic Dunkirk evacuation from 26 May to 4 June 1940, one-tenth of the BEF had been taken prisoner and several thousand evaders had been left behind in France. To make matters worse, an increasing number of downed RAF aircraft over the newly occupied continent swelled the number of evaders roaming as discreetly as possible in France. 'Most headed for Vichy France, as did most of the early escapers; and there the authorities concentrated as many of them as it could lay hands on in fortress internment at Marseilles. On 6 August 1940, Menzies, [Stewart Menzies, Head of MI6] no doubt with Dansey's approval [Colonel Claude Dansey, Assistant Chief of MI6], saw Crockatt and made him a proposition. MI6 offered to set up an escape line to run from Marseilles into Spain.'[23] This was the first of many escape lines formed and operational during World War II.

By the end of the war a number of legendary, ingenious and perilous escape lines had been set up to get evaders back to Britain. The Comet Line (so called because of the speed at which it operated), The Shelburn Line and The Pat Line were just three that enabled hundreds of soldiers and airmen to make their way back to Britain. All the escape lines existed in co-operation with local Resistance movements, and for the brave men and women of these various groups it was a dangerous and deadly form of collaboration. They were constantly at risk of discovery, betrayal and brutal retribution from the Nazis. Countless people lost their lives helping the escapers and evaders, but without them any plan by MI9 was doomed to failure.*

At the beginning of the war, the prospect of becoming an escaper or evader seemed remote to the new recruits. The bravado and confidence of British soldiers, sailors and airmen was such that many refused to countenance the idea of becoming a prisoner or having to evade the enemy on foreign soil. As M.R.D. Foot observed, 'A constant difficulty with combat aircrew was to persuade them that capture was not merely a remote possibility but a daily fact…' and that, on the high seas, '…Admirals were particularly stubborn in refusing to allow their crews' time to be wasted, as they saw it, in a piece of training hardly likely to be relevant to a sea career.'[24] But as the war progressed, particularly once the trauma and tragedy of Dunkirk began to sink in, so the very real prospect of being on the run from the enemy had to be expected.

Fortunately, as far as the air force and the army were concerned, the lectures laid on by MI9 and given by

---

* 'Over 500 civilians from France, Belgium and Holland were arrested and shot or died in concentration camps. A far greater number succumbed to their treatment after the war.' *Saturday at MI9*, Airey Neave (Hodder & Stoughton, 1969)

escapers and evaders from World War I were presented to 'young, eager men, under-informed about war, anxious to learn; angry at the political trap that had snapped around them, making them fight Nazism instead of pursuing some more peaceable career; and brought up on a different set of unspoken assumptions from those that governed the minds of their elderly commanders. Many of them had read such books as *The Escaping Club*, and the concept of escape as a quasi-romantic adventure was one that they could readily seize.'[25]

These lectures impressed on the young soldiers and airmen that it now became a duty for all ranks – not just commissioned officers – to try to escape. Whilst those captured at Dunkirk, or on the run in France following the retreat, consisted mainly of soldiers, as the war progressed the majority of escapers and evaders were aircrew. And the return of downed aircrew to Britain was vital in the war effort. MI9 also set about devising ingenious tools, maps, compasses and weapons that could assist any escaper or evader. The man behind this operation was Clayton Hutton, universally known as 'Clutty', one of the first six officers to join MI9 at the Metropole Hotel and a veteran of World War I. 'His enthusiasm was as unlimited as his ingenuity and his capacity for getting into trouble with the staid authorities of service and civilian officialdom.'[26] In his autobiography, Hutton highlights this side of his personality by quoting a letter that his boss, Crockatt, sent to an army provost marshal: 'This officer [Hutton] is eccentric. He cannot be expected to comply with ordinary service discipline, but he is far too valuable for his services to be lost to this Department.'[27]

On joining MI9, Hutton got the British Museum to gather as many books as they could find about true World War I escapes from the second-hand bookshops around Bloomsbury. He then tasked pupils from Rugby School's sixth form to summarise them, and from these summaries he observed the critical need for maps. Obtaining a supply of silk from a friend, he teamed up with Bartholomew's in Edinburgh and began producing maps printed on silk using pectin. Soon, most operational aircrew involved in missions over Europe carried with them a small silk map of Germany, roughly 18 inches square and, later, a series of maps disguised as playing cards was introduced. He then devised luminous compasses that could be hidden in a pipe, fountain pen, buttons or a cap badge, often hidden by a layer of paint that could be scraped off when the compass was needed.[28] Then came the escape box, a small package the size of a cigarette pack that would fit into the map pocket of battledress trousers and contained malted milk tablets, boiled sweets, a bar or two of plain chocolate, matches, Benzedrine tablets for energy, Halazone tablets for purifying water, a rubber 1-pint water bottle, a razor with magnetized blade (to act as an emergency compass), a needle and thread, soap and a fishing hook and line, which could also be used as makeshift braces or, in the case of injury, as a sling. These boxes became standard issue from the autumn of 1940 in the RAF and two years later in the USAAF, and were also accompanied by a coloured purse containing currency for any country that was to be flown over, a small brass compass and the relevant silk map.

By June 1940 the first evaders were returning to Britain alongside those evacuated from Dunkirk. Some of these evaders had made their own way to Spain, but by the end of 1941 most of them crossed the Pyrenees to the sanctuary of San Sebastian in the Basque Country or Barcelona in the east of Spain with the aid of the first organised escape lines. Once across the border, they'd be handed over to British consulates before being transferred to the British Embassy in Madrid.

At this point in the war, MI9 had created a well-defined method of evasion for downed airmen: get away undetected from the aircraft and enter a system of safe houses. Here, the owners would hide and feed you until couriers would take you to a collecting point in towns and cities such as Amsterdam, Brussels, Paris, Marseille or St-Jean-de-Luz. Given false papers and civilian clothes, you would then be taken to a frontier zone and be led by local guides over the mountains and into Spain.

The two famous escape lines into Spain were the Pat Line, which passed through Barcelona, and the Comet Line, which went through Bayonne and San Sebastián. Although the figures cannot be clarified, it is estimated that over 1,600 Allied evaders made their way back to Britain to resume the war effort via these lines. Throughout, despite the involvement of MI9, it was the locals who carried the greatest risk, the dark threat of betrayal constantly hanging over these escape lines with the Gestapo waiting to pounce.

THE AGENCY

It is thought over 500 civilians died in the cause of the escape lines, 150 alone being betrayed by the English traitor Harry Cole.

Born in 1903 in the slums of London, Cole was a petty thief by the time he was a teenager and prior to the outbreak of World War II had served time in prison for a number of offences including embezzlement and cheque fraud. Lying about his criminal past he was able to enlist in the British Army and was sent to France as part of the BEF. In May 1940, Cole was arrested for stealing money from his own sergeant's mess and found himself a POW when he was left behind after his unit pulled out during the fall of France. Managing to escape, Cole ended up in Lille, proclaiming himself to be a captain in the British Secret Service. Popular with women, and with an undying love of money, he had a military moustache and was always smartly dressed, usually wearing a regimental tie. When in Lille he would speak French with a pronounced British accent and carried with him at all times a letter certifying that he was deaf and dumb. He would produce this letter whenever approached by Germans and pretend to use sign language to deter any questioning.

For a number of months Cole organised a reliable escape line for Allied evaders from Lille, but he was beginning to arouse the suspicions of Captain Ian Garrow and Pat O'Leary (in reality a Belgian doctor, Dr Albert-Marie Guérisse) in Marseille because he was also stealing money from the escape organisation. O'Leary had Cole watched and it was clear that he was not all that he claimed to be. A meeting was arranged, Cole was arrested and locked in a bathroom while O'Leary and others deliberated his fate. However, Cole managed to escape and handed himself over to a branch of the German Military Intelligence. Within days he betrayed two of his most loyal helpers in Marseille and shortly afterwards gave the Nazis a thirty-page document of names and addresses of Resistance members. Using other aliases, and working for the Nazis, Cole was often present when those he betrayed were arrested, the Nazis often 'arresting' him too so his treachery would remain undiscovered. Of the 150 French people he betrayed, it's thought that 50 were killed.

Cole was eventually captured masquerading as an English captain called Mason in 1945 while working for the Americans in their Counter Intelligence Corps, a job he used to denounce his former Gestapo colleagues in an effort to cover his tracks. It was one of Cole's mistresses who exposed him to the Americans, and he was arrested and brought to Paris. But using the cunning he had employed with such deadly proficiency, Cole managed to persuade his guards that he should be allowed to write his memoirs in the guard room. As soon as his guards took their eyes off him, he slipped away in a stolen American sergeant's jacket. Hiding above a bar in Paris, after the war had ended, Cole was eventually discovered during a routine police search on 8 January 1946. Cornered, he drew a pistol and fired at the police, wounding one of them. Returning fire, they shot him dead. The man who identified Cole's body was none other than Pat O'Leary who had just been liberated from Dachau concentration camp, where he had been interred since an associate of Cole betrayed him in March 1943.[*]

While the Pat Line was being compromised by Cole, the Comet Line also suffered as the Germans focussed strongly on the evaders and their local helpers. Created by twenty-four-year-old commercial artist Andrée (or Dédée) de Jongh in 1940, the Comet Line helped over four hundred Allied soldiers escape through occupied France to Spain and Belgium, with Dédée herself escorting 118 airmen over the Pyrenees. At first, MI9 were reluctant to trust Dédée when she turned up at the British Consulate in Bilbao with three evaders whom she had just helped over the mountains and explained her plan to help more British servicemen escape across the Pyrenees, in exchange for out-of-pocket expenses.

'I was very impatient to do something,' she recalled. 'A woman couldn't carry a gun or fly a bomber jet, but she could walk unnoticed, striding down a street in a wool coat and sensible shoes as if on her way to the market or a typist's job, trailed quietly by two or three wayward soldiers in disguise.'[29] It turned out she had been inspired by the story of Edith Cavell, the British nurse shot at dawn in Brussels by the Germans in World War I for helping hundreds of Allied soldiers escape from occupied Belgium, although

---

[*] Cole's wife, Suzanne Warenghem, refused to identify his body. She had assisted evaders from Dunkirk earlier in the war and worked for the Pat Line. She married Cole on 10 April 1942 and gave birth to his son, Alain Patrick, in October 1942 but the baby died in January 1943 because Suzanne was in hiding in Marseilles after Cole betrayed her to the Gestapo and couldn't afford to feed him. She was eventually taken to England from Brittany on 26 February 1944, with the Gestapo hot on her heels, where she lived after the war. She told friends that when she died she wanted her ashes spread from an aircraft over England. That is what happened upon her death.

Dédée appeared totally unaware of Cavell's secret career as an intelligence agent.*

Amongst the consulate staff in Bilbao there was a suspicion she might be an infiltrator or a German agent; after all, it was difficult to believe that this slight and seemingly ordinary young woman could swim rivers, cross mountains and guide Allied airmen past German patrols. Back in London, Crockatt decided she warranted a proper investigation, and she was given the all clear. 'Bilbao, with patience and skill, replied that in the judgement of those who had met her, she was a girl of radiant integrity, as well as something of a beauty, and physically hard as nails – otherwise she could never have managed the mountain crossings, and it was established she had not been smuggled in by the geographically easy way, by Irun or Fuenterrabía from Hendaye.'[30]

The stamp of approval came when Dédée met Michael Creswell, a young diplomat working as an attaché in Madrid and known within MI9 by the codename Monday. He was captivated by her intense and forceful personality and MI9 sanctioned her line – but on the firm basis that she was to concentrate her efforts only on the repatriation of British

---

* The German claim that Cavell was a spy was vehemently denied by the British government at the time and she became a national heroine whose death inspired tens of thousands to join up for the war effort. However, new research has indicated that Cavell was working with the intelligence services and that MI5 was anxious to suppress anything that would implicate her in spying. Stella Rimmington, the former head of MI5, said in 2015 after researching Belgian archives: 'Her main objective was to get hidden Allied soldiers back to Britain but, contrary to the common perception of her, we have uncovered clear evidence that her organisation was involved in sending back secret intelligence to the Allies.' Richard Maguire of the University of East Anglia goes further: 'Cavell was not merely acting as a nurse and treating the wounded – she could have done this without helping those soldiers to then escape.' He added: 'I think we now have to accept that the likelihood is that Cavell was working for British intelligence, or at the very least was happy for the network to be used for its purposes.' *Edith Cavell: Shot by Germans. Celebrated 100 Years On*, Richard Norton-Taylor (*The Guardian*, 12 October 2015)

airmen. 'MI9 had suddenly discovered a real purpose for itself. The Cinderella organisation had its invitation to the ball and, though it would never achieve the superstar status or the glamour of, for example, SOE [Special Operations Executive], nor attract huge resources of money or staff, it was nevertheless now firmly established with a job to do. Until then the rescue of men from occupied Europe had been largely humanitarian – and that purpose was running out as the number trapped in Marseilles dwindled. The emphasis switched. Now MI9 was seen as having an important and utterly pragmatic contribution to make to the war.'[31]

Given the codename Postman, Dédée made more than 30 double crossings and escorted 118 evaders, including more than 80 aircrew. She had strict rules for those she helped escape: they had to walk at least 15 feet behind her at all times and never to speak in public – not to her, to one another, not to anybody. And she gave any airman who had a friendly face that might encourage a stranger to initiate a conversation a copy of *Le Figaro* and instructions to keep it hoisted, as if reading it, while she gave others oranges with the instruction to peel them messily every few hours on a train journey to repel any inquisitive neighbours.

However, on 15 January 1943 Dédée was betrayed. Sheltering in a house at Urrugne in south-west France with three RAF evaders she was arrested when the house was stormed. 'The door burst open and the barrel of a Schmeisser machine gun poked through. I'd seen one in a film but never in real life. My heart started pounding and I was really afraid. This was it. It was over for me, all over,' she recalled. 'I put my hands up. I remember it to this day, all as if it was in slow motion. They took us downstairs, lined us up against the wall and told us we were to be shot as saboteurs. I was resigned to dying.'[32]

A local farmhand had incorrectly thought that Dédée and her colleagues were making money out of the escape line and wanted his share of the spoils. When they refused he went off and told the authorities. It was a calamitous moment for the Comet Line but, despite her suffering brutal interrogation twenty times at the hands of the Gestapo, they refused to believe her confession that she alone was the line's leader and its mastermind: 'Don't be ridiculous,' her Nazi interrogators said.[33] Sent to Ravensbrück concentration camp, she endured hardships, starvation and brutality so intense that when the Gestapo looked for her for re-questioning she was so skeletal that they could not recognise her.*

Incredibly, without Dédée the Comet Line was rebuilt. But less than six months later it was infiltrated by a German agent with equally devastating effects, including the arrest of Dédée's father, Frédéric de Jongh.

Jean Masson was a twenty-five-year-old Belgian, the illegitimate son of a doctor. His real name was Jaques Desoubrie and, eagerly accepting the Nazi doctrine as a teenager, he joined the Gestapo in 1941. In the spring of

---

* After the war, Andrée de Jongh was decorated by King George VI and honoured by the American and French governments. In Belgium, she was named a countess. She waved off most of the attention and strived instead for a purposeful sort of invisibility, spending twenty-eight years nursing in a leper colony in the Belgian Congo and at an Ethiopian hospital. She died on 13 October 2007 aged ninety.

1943, Masson came into contact with the leaders of the Comet Line and de Jongh thought him suitable as a guide. On 15 May, Masson was ordered to Brussels to collect some airmen, bring them to Paris and deliver them to 'Franco',* the head of Comet. When he arrived at the Gare du Nord with seven airmen he was greeted by, amongst others, de Jongh. Satisfied with Masson's work, de Jongh and fellow Comet Line operative Robert Aylé gave him more jobs. Little did they know they had just hired one of the most notorious traitors of World War II.

On just his second trip less than a month later, Masson betrayed de Jongh in Paris along with six airmen and two other members of Comet, including Aylé and his wife. To protect his role, Masson was also arrested and taken to the Gestapo HQ on the Rue des Saussaies in handcuffs. But Masson was conspicuous by his absence in the police cell. Had he been taken off to be interrogated? Had he been shot trying to escape? The brutal truth emerged when the door to the cell de Jongh was sharing with Aylé and his wife opened. There, standing before them, was Masson, handcuffs removed and a sinister smile on his face. His first words to them were, 'Well, you fools', before spitting on the floor in front of them. 'Madame Aylé felt his face to be the most unpleasant she had ever seen. It was repellent in its triumph.'[34]

In danger of his true identity being discovered, the Germans kept Masson hidden until the end of 1943 when he reinvented himself as Pierre Boulain and proclaimed

---

* 'Franco' was a twenty-three-year-old Belgian called Baron Jean-François Nothomb.

that not only had he previously worked for de Jongh but he had also been responsible for the liquidation of Jean Masson. While de Jongh and Aylé were executed by firing squad in Paris on 28 March 1944 following their betrayal, Desoubrie – whether as Jean Masson or Pierre Boulain – continued to infiltrate escape lines and Resistance groups, and was responsible for over 160 Allied airmen being arrested as well as the internment or deaths of an unknown number of Resistance operatives, including 'Franco' in January 1944. Eventually arrested by the Americans, Desoubrie was tried and executed in Lille in 1949, his final words being '*Heil Hitler*'.[35]

Following the arrest of 'Franco' in early 1944, it was obvious that the Comet Line had a traitor somewhere in its midst. It couldn't have come at a worse time: with the increase of bombing raids over Europe in the run-up to D-Day, more and more downed airmen were finding themselves on the run and desperate to get back to Britain. But the perilous nature of the Comet Line was not the only obstacle facing airmen trying to return home. The bombing runs by RAF Bomber Command and the US 8th Air Force over occupied France had become more intense as the Allies attempted to disrupt communications in preparation for the imminent D-Day invasion in Normandy. This significantly affected the railway network, which the escapers were dependent on to get from Paris to Spain. It left these airmen exposed and at risk with seemingly no way out. The Comet Line did what it could, fitfully, but the savage bombing made it unsafe to take more than a few airmen from Paris. 'It was not worth the risk. Orders came from London to concentrate the men in groups in Belgium and Central France,' wrote Neave.[36]

However, unbeknown to the downed airmen, a plan for them was already underway, one that seemed audacious almost to the point of madness but was, at the same time, brilliant in its simplicity.

At the heart of the plan was a twenty-eight-year-old army officer deep within MI9 who had already made himself a nuisance to the Nazis and who was about to pull off the greatest evasion operation of World War II; a man with his own recent experience of escape and evasion, a man later referred to as 'the ghost in the establishment'.[37]

CHAPTER 6

THE MAN BEHIND THE PLAN

'Lying half-conscious on my bloodstained stretcher in the tunnel, I saw the shadow of a large figure in German uniform leaning over me. I remember now most vividly the sense of peace after the shattering roar of battle. Until this moment the fight had raged without respite in the blazing streets.'[38] This was how Lieutenant Airey Neave recalled his capture in Calais on 26 May 1940. Serving in the Second Battery of the 1st Searchlight Regiment, Neave had been amongst the 3,000 British and 800 French soldiers who had fought for four days against hopeless odds as Calais burned around them.

It was a hellish end: he remembered the wounded crying out for water, he described survivors emerging from burning houses and trenches with bullet wounds hastily bandaged and their white, unshaven faces showing the strain of long bombardment, and he recalled seeing a young soldier blow his brains out rather than surrender. Now, wounded himself, and as the miraculous evacuation of 330,000 men of the BEF at Dunkirk took place without him 27 miles to the east, Neave was to begin what might have been the end of his war; taken prisoner, spending the next six weeks in hospital and then being imprisoned in the impregnable Colditz Castle in Saxony after a failed escape attempt at Bydogszcz in Poland. But far from ending his war, Neave's capture merely kick-started it. Up to that point, his foray into World War II had seen him do little more than operate searchlights in the fields around Boulogne, but he had been studying for war for most of the thirties and, as the war progressed, it would come to define Neave's life.

Airey Neave was born in Knightsbridge, London, on 23 January 1916 to Sheffield Airey Neave, a naturalist and entomologist who had spent many years working in East Africa, and his wife Dorothy. Shortly after he was born, the family moved from London and settled in Beaconsfield, Buckinghamshire. His early life was comfortable, the family were descended from bankers and doctors, fortunes had been inherited and upward mobility was a characteristic streak running through his forebears.

At nine years old, Neave was sent away to prep school in Sussex. He failed to distinguish himself there, but it didn't prevent him from gaining access to Eton, his father's old school, at the age of twelve. Whilst at Eton, Neave was no more than a competent scholar but was exposed to activities such as shooting, fencing and even signalling when he enrolled in the school's Officer Training Corp.

However, in 1933, while he was still at Eton, Neave's parents sent their seventeen-year-old son on a trip abroad. Its function, ostensibly, was to enable him to pick up a foreign language, but they had little idea that his autumn trip to Germany would instead offer him a glimpse of the rise of fascism and encourage him to prepare for a conflict that few at that stage saw coming.

Arriving in Nikolassee in south-west Berlin in September 1933, Neave found a country swept up with Nazi fervour. As a result of the Enabling Act being passed in both the Reichstag and Reichsrat on 24 March 1933 all parties in Germany, with the exception of the Nazis, were banned or forced to dissolve. Consequently, Hitler and his cabinet were now ruling Germany by emergency decree, even though Paul von Hindenburg remained president.

Neave stayed with a local family and attended lessons at a nearby school. By now all German schoolchildren were expected to begin the day in their classroom with the Nazi salute, though Neave was exempt being a foreigner. He remembered being invited to take part in a festival of sport that involved a march through Berlin during the late evening. Initially, the march began in a light-hearted vein but 'As we joined the uniformed Nazis with their band, our mood changed. I felt as if I was being drawn into a vortex.'[39] Farther into Berlin they marched, by now behind the *Sturmabteilung*, the original paramilitary wing of the Nazi party, past enthusiastic, almost hysterical crowds of onlookers, past the burnt-out remains of the Reichstag as bands played '*Horst-Wessel-Lied*', the Nazi anthem, and onlookers gave the Nazi salute with purpose and vigour. 'Some were on the verge of tears,' Neave later wrote. 'Afterwards I realised that they were lost forever to the Revolution of Destruction, whereas I would escape.'[40]

Returning to Eton towards the end of 1933, Neave wrote a prize-winning essay examining the likely consequences of Hitler's rise to power in Germany and predicting the outbreak of war in Europe in the near future.

From Eton, Neave went to study law at Merton College, Oxford, where one of his classmates was Leonard Cheshire, who would go on to become one of the most highly decorated pilots in the RAF during World War II. He also observed the nuclear bombing of Nagasaki before dedicating the remainder of his life to supporting disabled people and lecturing on conflict resolution. Cheshire recalled Neave being an independent young man during his time at Oxford: 'No matter what the opposition, he would often do things that were a little wild, though always in rather a nice way and never unkindly.'[41]

While at Oxford, Neave joined the Territorial Army (TA), although their activities at the time could hardly be categorised as being at the cutting edge of warfare. 'To be a Territorial was distinctly eccentric,' he wrote. 'Military service was a sort of archaic sport as ineffective as a game of croquet on a vicarage lawn and more tiresome.'[42] The TA did undertake occasional military exercises on the Wiltshire Downs, somewhat rudimentary in their nature, but Neave he found he could glean more information on conflict, warfare and military tactics by reading the works of the

Prussian general and military theorist Carl von Clausewitz rather than by taking part in imaginary manoeuvres led by weary soldiers from World War I. Cheshire recalled Neave nose-deep in such military-theory books whilst at Oxford, appearing to spend more time studying them than the actual law books for his degree. When asked why he bought and read the full works of Clausewitz he answered that since war was coming, it was only sensible to learn as much as possible about the art of waging it.[43]

By 1935, Neave had risen to the rank of a second lieutenant in the TA but rather than opt for a career in the military after Oxford he headed for London to read for the bar, beginning with a placement at a solicitor's in the City in 1938 before, a year later, joining a barrister's firm in the Temple.

Across the Channel the spectre of war was looming ever larger. Germany had annexed Austria and by March 1939 had occupied Czechoslovakia. The British government's policy of appeasement seemed redundant in the face of German advances and, on 29 March 1939, the Secretary of State for War announced that the TA was to be increased in size with immediate effect and eventually doubled in numbers. Less than a month later conscription was introduced for the first time in British peacetime history.

Neave heard the news of the increase in TA numbers on the radio and rushed to join up with his younger cousin, Julius. Entering the Drill Hall, they were greeted by a recruiting officer who asked, 'Would you like to be soldiers or officers? Julius remembered them answering, 'Given the choice – officers!'[44]

Neave spent the next few months posted to an anti-aircraft Searchlight Regiment undergoing training in Essex and Hereford as, across the Channel, the opening salvoes of World War II commenced. He was desperate to join the action. 'The operation of searchlights, however bright, is not, in my opinion, a shining form of warfare. It did not conform to my desire to be in the field with Rupert Brooke and other heroes of the past. It so happened that after six months in a muddy field in Essex, I was posted to a searchlight training regiment at Hereford. I had now become a "gunner", a very comprehensive term in the British Army.'[45] In February 1940, Neave finally got his wish for action when he was sent to France as part of an advanced party operating searchlights in and around the fields of Boulogne.

Less than three months later, however, Neave was caught up in the frantic retreat of the BEF as Hitler's Panzer divisions blazed their way towards the Channel coast. On 10 May 1940 they began overrunning Belgium. Soon they were striking into France and, on 15 May, the French prime minister, Paul Reynaud, woke Winston Churchill with an early morning telephone call. 'He spoke in English, and evidently under stress. "We have been defeated,"' recalled Churchill. 'As I did not immediately respond he said again; "We are beaten, we have lost the battle." I said: "Surely it can't have happened so soon?" But he replied: "The front is broken near Sedan; they are pouring through in great numbers with tanks and armoured cars."'[46] Two days later Churchill ordered his staff to draw up plans for the evacuation of the BEF from France, now surrounded, out-gunned and outnumbered, and in peril from the advancing German Panzers.

On 21 May, Neave found himself in the French farming village of Coulogne, a few miles south-east of Calais, operating as a troop commander in the 2nd Searchlight Battery. They had retreated from Arras, where two British tank battalions had launched a valiant counter-attack against Rommel's advancing German divisions. It was a David versus Goliath battle: 74 slow British tanks up against 218 faster, more powerful, better-armed Panzers. But, somehow, the British tanks managed to stop Rommel in his tracks for a short while.

'At one point, the British were causing such problems on Rommel's right flank that many of his infantry and artillery fled. It was only when Rommel personally dashed between his tanks and guns – sometimes on foot – that German order was maintained.'[47] The impact of the British counter-attack brought time for soldiers heading to the French coast desperate to get back to Britain. Despite the bravery of the counter-attack, local refugees failed to appreciate the flight of the British soldiers, as Neave was to experience first-hand: 'As we approached the medieval town of Ardres, 10 miles south of Calais, a woman spat at us and called us cowards. She shook her fist and shouted: '*Merde!*''[48] In Coulogne, Neave and his seventy men were expected to defend the town against the might of Rommel's Panzers with rifles, two Bren guns and one Boys Anti-tank Rifle 'which no-one had, as yet, been trained to fire'.[49]

Expecting to die, Neave was nearly killed when a mortar exploded nearby, showering him with broken tiles and branches and killing his despatch rider. Despite being totally out-gunned, Neave's men managed to hold the advancing Germans for five hours before being given the order to withdraw to Calais. As they travelled, Neave could see plumes of smoke rising from nearby Dunkirk where hundreds of thousands of men had gathered to be rescued and where the 30th Infantry Brigade had just arrived from Britain to help thirty-nine-year-old Brigadier Claude Nicholson hold off the Germans, so giving more time for the evacuation on the beaches.

On 24 May, Neave and his men did what they could to defend Calais from the increasingly incessant German advance, but it was a forlorn task. As the battle raged about him, Neave was ordered to move to the east side of the town. The sun was beating down, the pavements burning the soles of his feet. He hugged the walls of houses, cafés and shops as bullets ricocheted about him. He spotted an ancient British tank firing farther up the boulevard and then slowly move away. 'As it gingerly withdrew, I felt a sharp blow in my side. I crawled a few yards. I felt the blood running down inside my clothes and trickling to my stomach,' he remembered.[50] Managing to pull himself up, the owner of a local café brought him a large cognac while his wound was inspected by a medical orderly. 'You're a lucky one, sir. 'Arf an inch from the 'eart. Only a flesh wound,' the bespectacled orderly assured him.[51] Neave had actually suffered a 'penetrating flank wound' and was taken to the Hospital Militaire despite his protestations, concerned that he would be captured.

Undergoing an operation to treat the wound, Neave regained consciousness only to hear Stukas bombing the town. Soon the Germans were overrunning Calais. Those who could leave had done so and the evacuation farther up the coast at Dunkirk had ended. Not willing to be captured, Neave decided to make a break from the hospital. Crawling out into the street, he found scenes of devastation. Escaping a near miss from a shell that landed close by and which killed a colonel who was trying to escape with him, he was forced to take cover in a tunnel near the port. By the afternoon, the British had surrendered, Brigadier Nicholson was taken prisoner and the Germans were sweeping through the town. In the tunnel there was no further escape for Neave and soon the doors opened. 'A field grey figure appeared, shouting and waving a revolver. Then a huge man in German uniform and a Red Cross armband put me gently on a stretcher. I was a prisoner of war.'[52]

Wounded, a prisoner and en route to Lille, Neave's mind was already working overtime planning his escape. But while his mind might have been active, he was physically traumatised from his wound and his energy had been sapped. A chance presented itself to flee early on when the lorry carrying him and other wounded soldiers broke down, but he was incapable of taking the opportunity. Not only was he frail but, like virtually every other soldier or airman at that time, he had received no military training in the art of escape or evasion.

Following a period of treatment in a hospital in Lille, Neave and other captured officers were then incarcerated in Oflag IX-A at Spangenburg, a castle standing high above the town. It was a tough period for Neave, enduring not only the physical discomfort of winter with little warmth and meagre food but also the mental tribulations of imprisonment. 'For such imprisonment, there is a double tragedy. First there is the loss of freedom. Then, since there is no apparent crime to expiate, unless it be personal folly, a sense of injustice scars the spirit. This bitterness of soul has clouded the life of many a strong man.'[53]

In February 1941, Neave and some of his fellow prisoners were taken by train to Poland, apparently as a reprisal for the alleged ill-treatment of German officers in Canada. The new prison at Thorn (modern-day Toruń) was bleak, harsh and depressing; the only light relief the prisoners had from the cold, damp, cramped conditions and meagre rations was their nightly rendition of 'Abide With Me', sung as the sun set over the drawbridge above the moat. Imprisoned within the walls, with the expectation of spending the remainder of the war confined and unable to contribute, and barely existing in a building that had an air of death about it, Neave resolved to escape.

His plan revolved around a single wooden building where a captured British dentist worked. It was located in a part of the prison camp where NCOs and soldiers were confined, 4 miles from the officer's cells. Every Thursday, by a quirk of the German army's medical regime, officers were permitted to visit the dentist. For several weeks Neave would make a Thursday visit pretending he had inflamed gums. What he was really doing was planning his escape, realising he must leave nothing to chance. 'My plan was to escape from the dentist's quarters and conceal myself in the main camp where the men were lodged and in due time to escape from one of the groups of prisoners working in the open.'[54]

Neave spent his time stealing food for his escape, gathering civilian clothes from sympathetic outsiders and fellow prisoners and organising his reception in the main camp. His escape plans, which involved heading east towards Russia, had to be approved by the senior British officer in the camp, Brigadier Somerset. Despite some mocking of Neave's plan, it was agreed he should attempt his escape and he was paired up with a fellow escaper, flying officer Norman Forbes, a Hurricane pilot shot down in 1940 over the French coast and who spoke fluent German. On 16 April 1941, Neave and Forbes paid their visit to the dentist. A colleague had placed some bits of wood in a space beneath the roof of the lavatory, which they would carry to their new part of the camp to give the impression that they were NCOs and not officers. With a pre-arranged distraction from a fellow prisoner, Neave and Forbes were soon in the NCO compound. Knowing the Germans would quickly discover that two officers were missing, they remained concealed in the NCO's compound while their captors searched fruitlessly.

On the morning of 19 April, they joined a working party being sent outside the camp. Joining their colleagues singing 'Roll Out The Barrel', the two of them confidently marched alongside them undetected, then out of the gates and through the pine forests. They spent the day making paliasses (crude mattresses) until the coast was clear for them to hide in a barn. They stayed there until nearly midnight before escaping in stolen Polish civilian clothes, heading towards Russia with only their collected rations of tinned sardines and condensed milk to keep them going. By 8 am the following morning they had covered 20 miles. Keeping to fields to avoid the roads they pushed onwards to Włocławek, seeking shelter at night in Polish farmhouses (a risky venture as Hitler had transplanted German farmers into Polish farms) before finally arriving in Włocławek on, of all days, Hitler's birthday. Neave wrote: 'Hands were raised obediently in the Nazi salute by Poles and German nationals. We, too, saluted with a feeling of tired amusement.'[55]

By the third day of their escape Neave was physically exhausted but still managed to reach Warsaw the following day, and then on towards the Polish border with Russia. Despite their exhaustion the escape had, so far, gone well. However, as they approached the border they were conscious they had no papers. Greeted by a Polish woman in a rundown village they asked her where the frontier was. 'It is here,' she exclaimed before disappearing. Ahead of them they saw frontier posts and an open gate standing beside what appeared to be a deserted guardhouse. Perhaps their euphoria got the better of them, or maybe it was the physical and mental strain they had been through on the journey, but momentarily Neave and Forbes let their guard down. It was all that was needed.

Passing through the frontier posts they walked straight into two German sentries. With no papers Forbes did the best he could to talk themselves out of their perilous predicament, but it was no good. The suspicious Germans separated the two escapees and Neave found himself in the guard house being interrogated by another German, a 'hard-faced man'. Tired, anxious and confused, what little knowledge Neave had of the German language deserted him. He tried to distract his interrogators for as long as possible in the vain hope that Forbes might break away outside. When he could go on no longer, Neave produced his metal identity disc with his name on it and the words, 'Prisoner of War No. 1198'. Forbes was brought back into the room and the German delivered his ominous verdict: 'We don't believe you! You are not Englishmen, but Polish spies. This is a matter for the Gestapo.'[56]

Taken to a nearby village, they were interrogated separately before being placed apart in cells in a 'severe modern prison'. Above Neave's door were the words 'Airey Neave. Spy'. Surviving on a diet of foul turnip soup and bread ladled out by a Polish boy, Neave feared the worst from his captors, knowing that once in the hands of the Gestapo that was probably it. His mood wasn't helped when, one evening, the boy told Neave sadly, 'You are going tomorrow.' Neave could see no way out. 'I closed my eyes and despair came over me like a great fog.'[57] The next morning, as the rattle of keys in his door woke him, Neave prepared for the worst. But instead of an appointment with the firing squad, he was informed he would be heading back to the prison camp at Thorn with Forbes.

Later that evening they were reunited with the other POWs at Thorn and, within a few days, Neave felt himself invigorated and refreshed despite his surroundings. He began writing letters home, carefully concealing details of his escape attempt and recapture and covertly describing his experiences. The remainder of the time he devoted himself to reading Victorian novels that would bring a sense of peace and home. But his new approach to prison life was about to be shattered when he was woken one night by a torch shining in his face. A burly German guard ordered Neave to 'Get up and be ready to move immediately. We have had enough trouble with you.' With Forbes and two others, Neave was led out of the prison camp. 'Where in hell are we going?' Neave protested to his guards. 'To the Bad Boys' Camp at Colditz,' came the response.[58]

CHAPTER 7

THE FIRST HOME RUN

Colditz is a small East German town in Saxony overlooked by a hill spur, on top of which, since the Middle Ages, has stood Colditz Castle. The first castle, towering over the Mulde River, had been built on the site during the late eleventh century for the German King Henry IV. In 1504, a large part of the castle was destroyed by an accidental fire and rebuilt over sixty years into a Renaissance-style castle before being allowed to deteriorate during the nineteenth century, when the castle was used as a workhouse to feed the poor and those under arrest. In 1829, the castle became a mental hospital for the incurably insane and remained as such until 1924.

In 1933, on seizing power, the Nazis converted the castle into a political prison for communists, homosexuals, Jews and others they considered undesirable. On 31 October 1938, the German *Oberkommando der Wehrmacht* commandeered the castle to be used as a special escape-proof prison, known as Oflag IV-C, for enemy officers and prisoners of war who, for some reason, warranted strict treatment and special observation. 'Among them were those who escaped but were re-caught and suspected of intending to escape again,'[59] wrote Major Pat Reid, himself a prisoner at Colditz and whose own escape from the castle formed the basis of the 1955 film *The Colditz Story*.

The Germans were convinced that Colditz was escape-proof; 90-foot-high walls rose skywards, it stood on impregnable foundations, had sheer precipices on three sides and on the fourth a dry moat over which a solitary bridge provided the only entry and exit points, guarded by German soldiers. By putting all the Allied escapers in one place – the 'Bad Boys' as they liked to call them – the Germans thought they could keep an eye on them for the duration of the war. But what they failed to realise was that by congregating them in one place they were effectively creating the perfect escape academy in which some of the brightest, most cunning and devious minds could create some of the most innovative and incredible escape attempts ever devised. As Reinhold Eggers, chief of security at Colditz, observed, 'In this castle, the prisoners had the interior lines of communication, and the initiative as well.'[60]

Neave arrived at Colditz on 14 May 1941. Immediately he realised this was a prison unlike any other: 'I felt the battlements close in, enfolding me, so that I looked around in fear. White faces peered at me from the windows and men in strange clothes paced up and down in the shadows.'[61] He was soon to find, however, that everyone in the camp had only one thing on their mind: escape. Every minute of their incarceration was spent either pilfering and hiding items that could be used for an escape attempt, planning an escape attempt or baiting the 'Goons', their name for their German guards. Everybody worked to their strengths to facilitate escape, whether it was engineering, languages or map-making.

The first escape attempt while Neave was interred in Colditz happened in June 1941 when a party led by Reid attempted to tunnel out of the prison. However, they were betrayed by a German guard who had been paid 100 marks to conveniently look the other way. Instead, he informed the *Kommandantur* of the plan and the potential escapees were led away to a period of solitary confinement. Despite the failure of this plan, efforts continued to tunnel out of Colditz. Neave was one of the few who realised it was a futile task: 'I was early convinced that such puny efforts would be of no avail against the mass of rock. Escapers must pit their wits against a frailer element – the Germans themselves. The gap in their defences seemed to lie in the hope that the guards would be deceived in a bold attempt to leave by the front gate in German uniform.'[62]

In spite of his views that tunnelling was ineffective, he did help dig an international tunnel with British, French, Polish and Belgian officers using such random objects as broken knives, door latches and bits of metal stolen from the guards to hack away at the rock under their floorboards.

Neave knew it wouldn't work but felt any effort to escape strengthened the prisoners' spirits and discipline. Besides, he simply didn't want to be left out and it allowed him time to formulate his own escape plan, which consisted of him brazenly walking out through the front gate dressed as a German soldier. First, he had to get hold of one of the brass numbered discs that were held at the guardhouse and given to any visitor to Colditz, being returned when they left. In June 1941, Neave managed to acquire one of these discs from an elderly painter who was bribed with tobacco to convince the German guards he had lost it within the castle and then through ingenuity, bribes and the help of others, Neave somehow managed to fashion a German uniform over the next few weeks.

On 28 August, Neave took his chance. Under the cover of darkness, wearing his rudimentary uniform and carrying a makeshift rifle carved out of wood by a fellow prisoner, Neave managed to pass through the guardhouse thanks to the brass disc and some carefully selected and rehearsed German words. 'I felt again the sense of being free. It was like a drug that brought an intense pleasure, an exquisite unburdening of the soul. It equalled the moment when Forbes and I had first reached the artillery ground at Thorn and set off under the stars towards the east. I felt that I was acting in a theatre where no audience could hear me. My performance was for my own enjoyment. I smiled to myself and walked on.'[63]

But any euphoria that Neave felt was short-lived. The brass disc he had handed in at the guardhouse was No.

26, and the Germans had been told to look out for this missing disc. A vigilant sentry spotted it and called after Neave. Instead of stopping, Neave quickened his step. But, on hearing other German voices shouting at him from behind, he stopped and turned, caught in the glare of a German spotlight. It was a terrible mistake, the light picking out the sham nature of his fake uniform. Neave ran towards a row of bicycles but was ordered to stop. 'It was hopeless. I was not prepared to be shot for having failed so dismally,' he recalled.[64] He was given twenty-eight days in solitary confinement.

Undeterred, on his release Neave immediately set about planning his next escape and identified another potential route out of Colditz, a rough pathway sweeping down into the moat and up across the far bank before vanishing near the married quarters of the prison staff. 'A small wicket gate stood half open in the moat bridge wall. If he could gain access to this gate, he was free of the barbed wire, with only a fence round the married quarters and a 12-foot-high wall around the park beyond to negotiate.'[65] Unbeknown to Neave, Reid had also spotted this possible escape route (the Dutch later claimed they had spotted it even earlier), and had also worked out that the route began with a passageway that led to the attic on the upper floor of the guard house. Furthermore, Reid had discovered the passageway lay under the floor of the theatre. By chance. the Allied officers were about to begin rehearsals for their winter production, which could provide the perfect cover for any escape. Once again, it all depended on escapees disguising themselves as German officers in a much more convincing way than Neave's previous attempt.

Reid was convinced he could get four men out: Neave, another British officer and two Dutch officers (they left in teams of two, each with one Brit and one Dutch). So, on 5 January 1942, and now in possession of quite good fake German uniforms, Neave and Second Lieutenant Toni Luteyn were ready to go.

As snow lightly fell, Neave felt excited and confident. Once the *Appell*, the 9 pm roll call, was dismissed they hurried to the theatre with the other escapers and Reid. They carefully prised up the floorboards, slid down under the stage and cautiously crept along a passage towards the door that led to the guard house attic. Here they changed into their German uniforms as Reid worked at springing the lock. It took 10 minutes to open the door, the tension rising and their hearts pounding.

Reid ushered the four men into the room, shook hands and wished them good luck before locking the door behind them. They crept through the attic, with a wireless below them playing organ music. As the music got louder, the four took their chance, now going cautiously down some stairs, past the door to the officer's mess and down through the darkness into the passage beside the guard room. Through a half-opened door they got a glimpse of German uniformed guards inside. Then they headed out into the snow towards a sentry stamping his feet in the cold. They all saluted each other: things were going well. But without warning two German soldiers began following them, talking loudly. Neave recalls Luteyn growing tense, but it was the Englishman who nearly gave them away when he clasped his hands behind his back. 'March with your hands at your sides, you bloody fool,' whispered Luteyn.[66] The escapees passed beneath the clock tower, past a row of bikes, saluted the sentry and then found themselves at the wicket gate. They passed through, across the moat-bridge and went down into the moat.

It was snowing heavily now, and they were slipping and sliding. They began to head towards the married quarter when, to their shock, a German soldier emerged from the building and began heading straight towards them. 'He reached us, stopped and stared deliberately,' wrote Neave. 'I hesitated for a moment ready to run, but Luteyn turned on him quickly and in faultless German said crossly, "Why do you not salute?"'[67]

The admonished soldier did as ordered before moving on and leaving the escapees to struggle on down a steep bank to the outer wall. They clambered on top, rested a moment to catch their breath and then made the 12-foot leap. They were bruised, shaken and frightened. But they were out. With no time to lose they headed east towards the town of Leisnig where they planned to take a train to Leipzig, now pretending to be Dutch electrical workers, having discarded their uniforms to reveal a new disguise beneath.

Arriving on time, they boarded the 5 am train. Neave, exhausted from the exertions of the escape and seeing dozing workers all around him, fell asleep in the warmth of the carriage as the train trundled towards Leipzig. He was woken by a sharp kick from Luteyn, who remained awake and vigilant. Neave had started to mumble in English while dreaming. No one except Luteyn had noticed.

The train pulled into Leipzig at 6 am, but Neave and Luteyn were concerned to discover that their connection didn't leave until 8.52 pm. That meant they had to spend a whole day in Leipzig with nowhere to hide, shelter or sleep. They started in one of the stations' waiting rooms but here, once again, Neave almost gave them away when he pulled out a bar of Red Cross chocolate and began eating it. He attracted angry stares from those around him: no German had seen chocolate for months. 'To sit eating this forbidden delicacy in the waiting room of a great station made one not only an object of envy but of deep suspicion,' he recalled.[68] The two of them decided to leave quickly and wander around the city, find a bench to sit on and simply wait for their next train.

It was a strange experience for Neave: not only were countless German soldiers obliviously passing them close by but he had been imprisoned for months and this was his first taste of freedom with new sights, sounds and smells. He also witnessed the hopeless suffering of many of the citizens of Leipzig, hungry, shabby and worn out despite the city showing no signs of bombing. When a young girl sat next to Neave and attempted to strike up a conversation, they promptly left in case they gave themselves away. They found sanctuary in a cheap cinema and took their seats amongst German soldiers, sailors and their girls with a German officer sitting directly next to Neave. They watched a series of German propaganda films, which included a British plane being shot down and a British pilot being taken prisoner. It was distinctly uncomfortable viewing for the two escapees amongst a crowd of excited Germans.

When the lights came up, Neave and Luteyn made their way through the snow and blackout towards the station where they waited anxiously for their next train to Ulm. While in the waiting room, Neave could only glance nervously at the bullying SS men swarming through the station, elbowing civilians aside.

Finally boarding the train, Neave and Luteyn decided to stand in the cramped corridors of the carriage rather than risk having to entertain a conversation in a compartment. As the packed train made its way to Ulm, passengers disembarked at various stations, so making the two escapees seem somewhat conspicuous standing in the corridors when vacancies appeared in the carriages. The two men had seen one compartment that was occupied by a solitary figure – an SS officer. They shrank into the shadows of the corridor to evade his gaze but the door opened and he invited them to join him. To reject his invitation would have been risky so, with Luteyn doing all the talking in his perfect German, the two men entered the compartment. Feigning tiredness, Neave positioned himself in a corner and pretended to sleep (he couldn't actually go to sleep for fear of mumbling in English as he slept), but at least it meant the officer wouldn't speak to him. Luteyn convinced the German they were Dutch workers travelling to Ulm, and so convincing was his mastery of the language and his calmness that the officer even waved away military police who were passing through checking papers.

Early in the morning, the train pulled in at Regensburg, where the two escapees had to change trains. Bidding farewell to the SS officer, they boarded their next train and were soon travelling through the snowy Bavarian countryside. Arriving at Ulm, Luteyn attempted to buy two tickets to Singen, just north of the Swiss border. The girl behind the ticket desk became suspicious and demanded to see his papers before summoning the station police, who wanted to know why two Dutchmen, proclaiming they are in Ulm to work, would want to visit Singen.

Luteyn concocted a story saying they wanted to visit an aunt, but this didn't convince the police who sent them to the Labour Office across the square. Neave and Luteyn were ordered by a policeman up to Room 26 on the second floor. As there were no lifts, only stairs, the policeman was reluctant to accompany them: 'You go up there and fix your business, and I'll find you quarters,' he said.[69] The two of them couldn't believe their luck. Climbing to the top of the building they found an open window and were shortly back on the streets of Ulm. Soon they were crossing the River Donau and making their way to Singen, walking all night through freezing temperatures. After a close encounter with four German woodcutters, one of whom went off to fetch the police before Neave and Luteyn fled, the two escapees finally made it to Singen and the German-Swiss frontier. Avoiding the sentry on duty at a German control post, they scrambled across a snow-covered no-man's land. An hour later they heard the sound of cow bells and soon reached a road that led to Ramsen, a town in northern Switzerland where they were challenged by a Swiss frontier guard. Neave added, 'He was delighted that we had escaped the tyranny of Hitler and the street echoed with our cheering. Later that morning we were taken by Swiss police to Schaffhausen and placed under "hotel arrest". Eighty-four hours after my escape from Colditz, I was in the care of the British Military Attaché in Berne.'[70]

Granted three weeks rest at the home of a Swiss doctor near Gertenzee, Neave was then whisked back to Britain via Marseilles, over the Pyrenees, across Spain and into Gibraltar, where he boarded a troop ship that ferried him back to the Clyde. On 13 May 1942, Neave landed at Gourock, a small town in the west of Scotland.

Neave was the first Englishman to break out of Colditz and make it back to Britain. His escape was, essentially, a schoolboy tale of derring-do, a feat that played directly to the cherished wartime stereotype of jaunty British pluck. But, in reality, Neave wasn't the typical British hero and his escape is all the more remarkable for that. As Bruce Anderson wrote, 'Some warriors simply do not know the meaning of fear. Faced by threats, they charge. Others, like Airey Neave, have to summon up all their powers of resistance in order to screw their courage to the sticking place. They have to fight down doubts before they can confront dangers. That requires courage of a high order: Airey Neave's courage.'[71]

The other Englishman who escaped with Neave, Lieutenant John Hyde-Thompson, didn't make it. He and his Dutch escaper were apprehended at Ulm less than twenty-four hours after Neave and Luteyn had passed through. Returned to Colditz, Hyde-Thompson was finally liberated in April 1945.

Immediately after his escape, and during his time in Switzerland, Neave was unaware that his actions had aroused the interest of MI9. The British Military Attaché in Berne, Colonel Henry Antrobus Cartwright, was using the posting as cover for his own role in MI9, gathering intelligence for the war effort and he immediately realised how useful Neave might be. In effect he was being talent-spotted and, during his debriefings in Berne, Neave provided Cartwright with valuable information that MI9 craved, information that only served to show his ideal credentials as a potential operative for MI9. As Paul Routledge wrote, 'Innocently or otherwise (probably otherwise), Neave was offering himself as a prime candidate for intelligence work. In his first contact with the secret world of the security services, he acquitted himself well and his performance was duly noted.'[72]

When it was confirmed by Cartwright to Neave during his debriefings in Switzerland that he would be going home to Britain it was with the words, 'MI9 have asked for you.' They were desperate for any help in their escape and evasion operations in Europe, getting downed aircrew back and into the air again.

Who better to recruit than the first English escaper from Colditz?

CHAPTER 8

THE NEW RECRUIT

When Neave arrived back in Britain he was ordered to go to the Grand Central Hotel at Marylebone for interrogation, a hotel he knew all too well from his pre-war days, drinking there until the early morning before catching the train back to Oxford. Now it was surrounded by sandbags and soldiers with rifles and fixed bayonets. Inside, the waiters and receptionists had disappeared, replaced by military policemen and orderlies.

'I was directed to the reception desk where two years before a splendid blonde in black had been on guard,' Neave recalled. 'Now there was a sergeant at the desk.

'"What is this place, Sergeant?"

'"The London Transit Camp, sir." He studied me politely.

'"Where are you from, sir?"

'"Germany."

'He did not bat an eyelid.

'"Quite so, sir. Then it will be MI9 you want. They are on the second floor."[73]

Entering a double bedroom that had been turned into an office, Neave found himself being interrogated yet again about his Colditz escape before he was informed that Captain Langley was waiting for him downstairs. Langley, once of the Coldstream Guards, had been captured at Dunkirk after being severely wounded. Neave had last seen him briefly in the hospital at Lille in the summer of 1940. Since then, Neave had been a prisoner of war and made his daring escape from Colditz while Langley had lost his left arm due to his wounds, before making a daring escape to Marseille where he had become acquainted with many of the early escape-line organisers. Shortly afterwards he was repatriated to Britain whereupon he began working for the security services.

When he entered what was once the downstairs lounge, Neave was greeted by Langley with the words, 'You made it. Congratulations,' before Langley told him that someone else wanted to meet him for lunch. It turned out to be Norman Crockatt, Head of MI9. Meeting at Rules in Maiden Lane, the oldest restaurant in London where, during World War II, anybody who was anybody in secret war work would meet and dine, Langley made himself scarce while Crockatt took his time delving into Neave's background and his knowledge, all the while seeing for himself whether this young man was suitable for a role in MI9.

THE NEW RECRUIT

Satisfied that Neave was just the man they were looking for, Crockatt said: 'Subject to your being cleared by the Security Service, I'm going to offer you a job. Would you like to work in our secret escape section with Langley?'[74] Neave needed no second invitation. 'That's the one job I should like to do,' he replied.[75] He was assigned the rank of Captain and would work in Room 900 in the War Office, the home of IS9(d)*. Warned that it wouldn't be bed of roses, Crockatt explained that he would be tasked with handling secret communications with occupied Europe and also be responsible for training agents. Shortly afterwards, Langley reappeared to inform Neave that he would be expected to build up an organisation of agents and helpers in Belgium and Holland.

Neave began work at MI9 on 26 May 1942, the second anniversary of his capture at Calais by the Germans. While most of MI9 worked from a house in Beaconsfield, Neave was based at the War Office. Choosing the codename Saturday†, he set about learning what he could about MI9, discovering quickly that it was an extremely professional organisation, if small, and that at virtually the outset of war it had begun setting up escape lines in Europe. He learned that MI9 gave lectures, often conducted by returned escapers or evaders, to British and Commonwealth servicemen (generally Allied aircrew), instructing them

---

* IS9 stood for Intelligence School 9, a department to which intelligence officers from all three services could go to be briefed on the intricacies of escape and evasion. As Paul Foot wrote: 'The symbol IS9 thus became widely known among fighting services and staffs and ... provided a convenient cover for MI9's field units later in the war.' *MI9: Escape & Evasion 1939–45*, M.R.D. Foot and J.M. Langley (Bodley Head, 1979)

† He also used the name Albert Hall to sign a number of micro-photographed messages to Brussels.

how best to evade capture rather than how to escape prison once caught. Their evasion naturally depended on the Resistance and, with the Pat Line and the Comet Line in full swing, for a couple of years everything seemed to be going well. Then, with the lines being infiltrated by Cole, Masson and others, many were betrayed and the lines compromised. This happened during the intensification of bombing runs over Europe as the Allied invasion plans for Normandy began to take shape. Consequently, more Allied airmen were being shot down over France, Belgium and Holland. It was these men that were in need of urgent rescue, to get them back into the war effort as quickly as possible.

By this point, not only had Neave married Diana Giffard, a fellow worker in the Secret Service,* but following Langley's promotion to joint commander of IS9 (Western European Area) he had also taken control of Room 900. It had undergone a particularly traumatic time in the months before Neave assumed the reins: the Gestapo had infiltrated the escape lines, the masterminds behind them – including Dédée and her father Frédéric De Jongh, Albert-Marie Guérisse (Pat O'Leary) and Jean Greindl – had either been arrested or killed while hundreds of other helpers had also been detained and incarcerated. The very existence of Room 900 had come under threat as the result of such disasters, and people were beginning to criticize their role, suggesting that military

---

* Diana Giffard began her war work as a nurse before being moved into Intelligence after being 'spotted' by a Foreign Office scout. Carrying out liaison work with the Polish government-in-exile's Ministry of Information, she focussed on propaganda, often in close co-operation with the BBC.

intelligence might be more valuable than escape work. But Neave had a retort: 'We protested that the saving of a bomber pilot's life could be as important as blowing up a bridge.'[76]

Crockatt shared Neave's philosophy and was determined to make MI9 a force to be reckoned with. Crockatt argued with the War Office that, despite the losses in the air, any airmen who evaded capture and had been returned to Britain were already back in the air and flying missions over Europe. Unsurprisingly, he received support for his argument from the Air Ministry. Neave couldn't understand any opposition to their plans to rescue evading airmen from Europe. 'I was aghast at the cynical belief that fighting men shot down by the enemy were of minor importance to other intelligence branches,' he later wrote.[77]

By now the situation was becoming desperate. The US had entered the war and joined in Allied bombing raids. This only meant an increase in the number of air crews being shot down over occupied Europe, and consequently the safe houses in Paris and elsewhere were becoming overcrowded, meaning more likelihood of their being discovered. With the Comet Line compromised and the O'Leary Line penetrated, Neave was told to come up with a new plan to get downed airmen back to Britain. Langley had formulated his own idea, a plan to evacuate men by sea from the coast of Brittany back to Britain. Organised by a team of French–Canadians working in tandem with patriots in Brittany, this route was named the Shelburne

Line*. It wasn't the first time MI9 had sought to evacuate by sea. In 1942 a number of evaders and escapers had been successfully evacuated from an area near Marseilles by the Royal Navy in two dramatic 'pick-up' operations with the help of Polish assistance, and as early as Christmas 1941 a bold but calamitous mission had sought to land food and provisions on the Glénan Islands off Concarneau for RAF escapers and evaders, although this mission ended in a fiasco.†

Excited by the prospect of the Shelburne Line going into operation, Neave flew from Bideford in Devon to Gibraltar in September 1943 with Colonel Cecil Rait, a senior MI9 officer, to discuss the way forward for escape and evasion practices with 'Monday' (Donald Darling) and 'Franco' (the Belgian, Baron Jean-François Nothomb). It was a

---

* The original name for the Line was Oaktree, but from the start it was compromised by a traitor within its midst. A German agent, Roger Le Neveu, betrayed those working in Oaktree and numerous arrests by the Gestapo in June 1943 decimated the organisation before any sea evacuations had taken place. In November 1943, plans for a sea evacuation from Brittany were resurrected. Two agents, Lucien Dumais and Raymond Labrosse, landed in the Oise Valley. Within days they had travelled to Paris to meet the French Resistance and then to the Breton town of Plouha to meet François Le Cornec, the local Resistance leader who took them to study the nearby coastline. Here they identified a shingle cove, Anse Cochat, as the ideal location for discreet night-time pick-ups. They codenamed it Bonaparte Beach. In January 1944 the first Shelburne Line evacuations took place. Originally scheduled for December 1943, bad weather had meant postponing the initial evacuation but eventually the coded message came through via the BBC News: *'Bonjour tout le monde à la maison d'Alphone'* ('Hello to everyone at Alphonse's house'). This was the green light they had been waiting for. On 29 January 1944, nineteen 'parcels' gathered in a small stone cottage a mile from the beach before being led down the cliff path in darkness. Once on the beach a French volunteer signalled in Morse code to the Royal Navy gunboat 503 waiting silently offshore. Seeing the signal, four rubber boats were dropped over the side and sailors and commandos rowed for the shore with muffled oars to collect their 'cargo'. At 9 am the following morning, the gunboat docked in Dartmouth with its fifteen evaders. The mission had been a success and the Shelburne Line was up and running. Over the next year the Line survived intact and flourished in secret. A total of 307 evaders were brought back to Britain, despite great risk.

† Sailing from the Isles of Scilly on Christmas Day 1941, the *La-Brise* was a mackerel boat fishing out of Newlyn in Cornwall. It had been taken over by a British crew for this mission, codenamed Anson, but ran aground on rocks at Ushant on the journey to Concarneau. Managing to extract her from these rocks the skipper, a RNR officer from Aberdeen allegedly drunk on whisky, was killed as a result of an accident with a box of hand grenades and the boat was eventually guided back to Falmouth by Lt. Daniel Lomenech, a Frenchman who had joined the Royal Navy and who knew the conditions on the Breton coast.

crucial meeting. Because of the infiltration of the Comet and Pat O'Leary Lines, it was imperative that an avenue of escape and evasion remained open for the downed airmen, especially with increasing air raids. The successful repatriation of these downed airmen was critical for the ongoing success of the war effort. However, the potential rewards of the Shelburne Line were yet to be recognised and, while the Comet Line still operated, it could not be relied upon. Besides, Neave's meeting in Gibraltar with Nothomb only too plainly revealed the conflict between the Belgians and the British.

The Belgians wanted the Comet Line to remain an independent French and Belgian Line, not one to be interfered with by the British (despite the fact that it was the British who had supplied the money to keep it functioning). In a tense conversation with Neave, 'Franco' questioned him forcibly: 'But the Line remains independent? A French and Belgian Line?' Neave replied, 'Yes, of course. We will respect that.'[78] After two days in Gibraltar, refreshed and satisfied that the Comet Line would remain independent, 'Franco' crossed back into Spain to continue his work and Neave flew back to London.

Returning to Britain and forbidden from entering occupied territory owing to strict wartime security, Neave was concerned he was not doing enough to help the Allied airmen hiding out or on the run in France, Holland and Belgium. Preparations for D–Day were well under way and Neave was anxious about the fate of the large numbers of escapers and evaders already on the Continent should heavy fighting increase following the invasion, as it undoubtedly would. Preliminary bombardment of rail lines, infrastructure and communications would make transit to a neutral country such as Spain virtually impossible. The Shelburne Line, regardless of any success it may have, would have to cease operations in March 1944 as the invasion grew nearer. Even without any further airmen being downed, it was estimated that 500 were already hiding in France needing repatriation. The prospect of them being caught in ferocious battlefields unarmed, exhausted and possibly wounded raised two scenarios: in the heat of battle could the advancing Allies really be expected to stop their advance to protect them and, perhaps more chillingly, would the retreating enemy look upon them favourably or exact bloody revenge as they fled? 'Over all of us hung the fear that if the Germans knew that they were losing the war, they would turn to brutal methods and spare no one, even in uniform,' wrote Neave.[79]

Following his trip to Gibraltar, Neave spent his time back in London either in Room 900 of the War Office or at Ebury House, 39 Elizabeth Street, near Victoria Station, the flat belonging to his wife's aunt, where he lived for the rest of the war, as well as using it as a makeshift office to interview agents. Here he contemplated what he could do to help the downed airmen. He had been given the responsibility for planning underground escape operations in the run-up to, and after, the D-Day invasion and was desperately concerned for the plight of these airmen. The exact date of the D-Day landings remained a closely guarded secret, but

THE NEW RECRUIT

Neave assumed it would be in the late spring of 1944. That didn't give him much time to develop and implement a plan. Wracking his brain, Neave pondered and plotted.

Finally, he hatched a plan. It was so brassy that few thought it could possibly succeed and most considered it too risky. But Neave was confident. He knew if he could surround himself with the right people, both in Britain and in France, it had a chance to succeed. It would depend on secrecy, planning and courage. If it worked, it would be a miracle. If it failed, a bloodbath.

Despite criticism, particularly from Crockatt, who feared a general massacre of Allied troops or airmen caught at large in occupied territory, and from the American W. Stull Holt,* Neave could think of no alternative. Operation Marathon, Neave's name for it, had to go ahead. And it could not fail. 'I knew that it was fraught with risk,' he added, 'but it was the best chance of saving these men from capture or summary execution as partisans.'[80]

---

* Holt (1896–1981) was an academic historian from Johns Hopkins University in Baltimore. He had previously served in World War I as a driver for the American Ambulance Field Service before joining the American Air Force and receiving his pilot commission as a first lieutenant. Working alongside Crockatt during World War II, Holt collaborated with MI9 to devise escape and evasion techniques for the US 8th Air Force that are still being used by the American military. His top-secret work earned him an Order of the British Empire from the British government and a Silver Star from the USA.

CHAPTER 9

THE PLAN

Operation Marathon was staggering in its simplicity. Neave's plan was to establish secret forest camps in the run-up to D-Day in heavily wooded regions, often right under the noses of the Germans, where evaders who could not be evacuated to Spain from Paris and Brussels could gather and hide until they were liberated by the advancing Allied forces following the invasion. It really was a case of hiding in plain sight.

Whilst they were in the camps, Neave planned that the evaders would be regularly supplied with food by airdrops in nearby fields and, if required, defended by the local Resistance forces. The proposed forest camps would be located in Rennes in eastern Brittany, Châteaudun to the west of Orleans and the Ardennes in Belgium. The locations would need to be sufficiently close to railway stations so that the evaders could be transported easily to them, and there would need to be well-organised Resistance groups nearby to help ferry the evaders to the camps, to assist in conveying food to them and protect them if necessary. 'I knew if we could find the right sites for the camps, it was the best chance of saving these men,' Neave later wrote.[81]

In the autumn of 1943, Neave began his preparations for Operation Marathon in earnest. With the Air Ministry giving him their total backing, he recruited a crack team of French and Belgian agents to lay the groundwork. He was unsure of numbers but estimated that up to four or five hundred evaders might require shelter in his forest camps and, consequently, it was imperative that he recruit the most highly trained and dependable team of organisers and wireless operators to carry out the plan. Amongst them were the Belgians George d'Oultremont, a tall, blond man who had already escaped from the clutches of the Gestapo in 1942, Baron Jean de Blommaert, one of the leaders of the Comet Line and known by the Germans as 'Renard' (the Fox), Albert Ancia and Squadron Leader Lucien Boussa, a Belgian in the RAF.

The group would meet discreetly at 22 Pelham Crescent, just off the Fulham Road in London, where d'Oultremont and de Blommaert lived. Here, in these civilised surroundings, the plans were put in place despite there being so much uncertainty about D-Day. The group had no idea when the landings would take place and no inkling when the invasion forces might reach the areas selected for the camps. This was critical as they would free the evaders within the camps, and Neave didn't want to risk them being in the forests for any longer than necessary as the Germans retreated.

Another problem facing Neave was the Comet Line. He knew it was necessary to work with Comet because it was ferrying downed airmen out of Paris, but he also knew that it was compromised and that any potential link needed to be conducted with the utmost discretion.

On 21 October 1943, d'Oultremont was parachuted into France with his French-Canadian wireless operator, Corporal Conrad Lafluer.* D'Oultremont had been a guide on the Comet Line until he himself had to cross the Pyrenees into Spain in December 1942 to escape the Gestapo. Now, travelling with false papers under the name of Laporte and carrying 3 million French francs, he landed near Reims. From here the two men had to find suitable landing fields for Lysander aircraft to collect agents and airmen, as well as contacting those high up within the Comet Line to begin planning the secure forest havens for evaders in France as D-Day approached. D'Oultremont also had to prepare for the arrival, again by parachute, of de Blommaert later the following month.

Travelling to Paris, d'Oultremont managed to recruit a number of French girls who would act as guides and a willing French banker who would look after the French francs before heading to Coucy-le-Château, where he found a potential landing site to evacuate agents and airmen.

---

* Prior to their departure, a party was held for them at the Embassy Club in London that went on into the early hours of the morning. That's when Neave heard that the Belgians had nicknamed him 'Napoleon'. So he suggested that Napoleon should be the codeword for the reception committee to identify new agents landing in France.

However, despite five airmen being safely evacuated at the beginning of November from this site, the Air Ministry were unenthusiastic about the operation and it was decided that d'Oultremont and Lafleur would be better employed making preparations for the camps as well as maintaining a parallel escape line to Comet.

At the end of November, de Blommaert was parachuted into France with Lemaître, a Belgian wireless operator, with the task of making new agents. De Blommaert had served with the Belgian Army until he was wounded just prior to Belgium capitulating in 1940. He joined the Resistance immediately and soon became one of the most daring figures in the Belgian Resistance, as well as an active organizer for Comet. His exploits quickly made him the scourge of the Nazis before he had to flee to Britain in 1942, whereupon he worked at 22 Pelham Crescent as part of the young Belgian group.

Neave identified de Blommaert as an 'exceptional organiser' with a reticence and thoroughness that commanded respect within the French Resistance. But no sooner had he landed in France than disaster struck. While he was making new agents, elsewhere in France the French-Canadian wireless operator Conrad Lafleur, who had parachuted in with d'Oultremont, suddenly disappeared from the airwaves. Back in London, Neave was preparing another parachute operation but now came the terrifying proposition that Lafleur had been captured and interrogated. Before it had even started Operation Marathon seemed to be under threat.

THE PLAN

As it happened, Lafleur had been betrayed by the husband of one of his couriers who had become a collaborator and given him away. One evening, Germans surrounded the house where Lafleur was transmitting and the Gestapo burst in, catching him red-handed on his radio. But as well as carrying 3 million French francs and copious amounts of cigarettes and whisky when they landed, d'Oultremont and Lafleur had also been well armed. Lafleur opened fire immediately, killing or wounding two Germans before jumping out of a window. Pursued by more soldiers, he threw a grenade at them before fleeing into the darkness. He escaped to a nearby town where, borrowing a black suit, hat and glasses from waiters at a local hotel, he evaded German police and boarded a crowded train to Amiens where a local physician hid him until the Comet Line arranged for him to be escorted to Spain.

Lafleur's escape left d'Oultremont without a radio operator so he made his way to Paris. Here, on 17 January 1944, he met 'Franco', now the head of the Comet Line. But a day later Nothomb himself was arrested when the traitor Masson resurfaced, this time under the guise of Pierre Boulain. Fearing the Gestapo were on his tail, d'Oultremont headed for Spain with new papers, but not before he had the chance to warn de Blommaert that he too was in danger. Hearing the news, Neave decided that he had to get de Blommaert out of France as quickly as possible to 'preserve all our best agents for Marathon and the invasion scheme'.[82] With Lemaître remaining in France, orders were given for de Blommaert to be evacuated. On

28 February 1944, Micheline Dumon* of the Comet Line handed de Blommaert the urgent message he was to return to Britain, and three days later he crossed the border with Conrad Lafleur into San Sebastián in Spain, where MI9 greeted them both before they were whisked safely back to England.†

Arriving back in Britain on 9 March, de Blommaert spent two days writing his report for Neave at his London home. Before he had left, Dumon had been able to provide him with a name of the traitor within the Comet Line – Pierre Boulain. Nobody at that moment realised that Boulain and Masson were the same man, but they knew the Gestapo were close to destroying the Paris element of the Comet Line. Knowing there was a traitor in their midst meant Neave was unsure whether he could risk sending de Blommaert back to France. Yet he knew that if he was to return, whatever the risks, and establish a camp in the countryside while keeping as far away as possible from Paris and Boulain, then perhaps he had every chance of remaining undetected and surviving.

At the outset of Operation Marathon, Neave had envisaged a series of small, mobile camps that would stretch to the Spanish border. The plan was for the evaders to leapfrog from camp to camp on bicycles or in lorries driven by local Resistance workers. But this was soon discarded.

---

* Micheline Dumon (1921–2017), best known as 'Michou', was actually Lilly Du Chalia. She had worked for the Comet Line since its earliest days, arranging shelter and providing guides for evaders to travel to Spain as well as creating false identity papers for airmen. She was forced to flee to London in May 1944. She was awarded the George Medal in 1967.

† Lafleur was awarded the Distinguished Conduct Medal for gallantry in the field and later became a truck driver in Toronto after the war. He died in 1979.

THE PLAN

The risks were too great. With the increase in targeted bombing by the Allies on the railway network in France more German soldiers than ever were having to travel by road. The potential for Allied evaders being discovered during transit was far too great.

Neave's next plan had been for three larger, static camps in Rennes, Châteaudun and the Ardennes. During discussions with de Blommaert, and with the knowledge that time was against them, Neave decided that one camp needed to be set up as quickly as possible. Together they scanned a map of the region around Chartres, Châteaudun and Orleans and decided on a forest area between Châteaudun and Vendôme known as the Forêt de Fréteval.

Fréteval Forest was thick with trees and a dense matted undergrowth. It was almost 300 square miles in size and situated 100 miles south of Paris. The only time it had warranted a mention in the history books prior to 1944 was when King Philip's soldiers skirmished with those of Richard the Lionheart in July 1194 as Richard returned from the Crusades. While Philip's men shadowed Richard's army as it moved through the forest, it appears that Richard doubled back on the French and ambushed them, causing King Philip to abandon his baggage train as he fled.

Now, 750 years later, it was the perfect place for Neave's proposed camp: it was only 10 miles away from the railway station of Châteaudun from where the local Resistance would transport evaders from Paris and other locations to the camp. It was also close enough to the Normandy beaches to ensure that liberation of the camp was likely to be fairly quick following the D–Day invasion, an important factor given the uncertainty concerning German retribution as they retreated.

There had been little Maquis* activity recently in the area, meaning that concentrated searches of the area by the Germans was less likely. In addition, the forest lay near an area of plains and farms, which meant a reasonable source of food for the evaders was guaranteed and decent areas in which parachute drops could occur. And crucially the forest also had a spring.

Despite everything going for it, however, there was one factor that couldn't be ignored. Three miles away was the small town of Cloyes. And stationed in Cloyes was a large deployment of German troops and a number of significant ammunition dumps. 'I was well aware that this plan, though original, involved great risks,' Neave noted.[83] But far from being daunted by the prospect of German soldiers being close to the camp, he saw it as an opportunity: would the Germans really think the Allies would hide hundreds of evaders right under their noses?

If Neave could get the evaders to Fréteval Forest from Paris and keep them there without them being discovered, he was sure he could pull off the greatest masterstroke of escape and evasion in World War II.

---

* The rural guerrilla bands of French Resistance fighters.

CHAPTER 10

OPERATION SHERWOOD

While the overall name of the plan to create up to three forest camps had been Operation Marathon, Neave decided to give the Fréteval Forest mission a specific codename, inspired by Britain's most famous forest-dweller, Robin Hood. So the plan became Operation Sherwood.

Back in London and with the site of the hiding place identified, Neave and de Blommaert diligently began putting the plan together. De Blommaert would be responsible for the Fréteval camp and Boussa (alias 'Cousine Lucienne') would be parachuted in to help him once the camp was ready.

First of all, Neave and de Blommaert had had to work out how they could discreetly but efficiently transport the evaders from Paris to Fréteval via Châteaudun. They would have to travel by train, but this was made all the harder following weeks and months of Allied bombing in the run-up to D-Day that had targeted, amongst other communication and transport networks, the French railways. The line from Paris to Châteaudun was still intact, but services were unreliable and when they did run they were often packed with German soldiers and still at risk of being bombed.

Furthermore, even if they could get the evaders safely from Paris to Châteaudun then they would have to be taken the final 10 miles to the forest along country roads randomly patrolled by Germans and with few hiding places should they meet the enemy.

Finally, if the evaders managed to make it to the forest, there was the challenge of keeping them fed and watered. The natural spring wasn't contaminated, and would provide a reliable water supply. Food, however, was a different problem. The location had been chosen because regular airdrops could be made nearby but landing supplies for the anticipated four hundred to five hundred men within the forest would be a perilous operation given the proximity of the German deployment in Cloyes and the potential for discovery. However, reports back from the area indicated that the Resistance movement was strong and active in the vicinity and that they also had the support of local farmers and priests. This suggested that locals supplying food to the evaders, even with meagre rations, would be possible until their liberation after D-Day.

'I could see that de Blommaert was excited by the prospect of this operation and that he believed it to be practicable,'[84] wrote Neave, who could also depend on

Albert Ancia working alongside them organising another camp in the Ardennes.

Neave came to the conclusion that, despite the risks of de Blommaert being discovered and captured, he would have to be sent back to France to explore and examine the forest and to form a relationship with the local Resistance. He would also have to recruit new agents in and around Cloyes. In addition, he would be tasked with diplomatically negotiating with the Comet Line as the evaders would be coming from them meaning, as a consequence, the Comet Line into Spain would effectively cease to exist. It was a precarious and delicate situation.

During his previous meeting in Gibraltar with Nothomb, Neave had been left in no doubt that the Belgians who ran the Comet Line didn't want it interfered with by the British. Added to this, a feeling of 'us-and-them' had inevitably surfaced between those who had 'stuck it out' in occupied Europe – such as the French and Belgians – and the British and Americans who had suddenly rocked up without having endured the deprivation and degradation of life in occupied territory with all it entailed. So how now would they react to the news of a British plan to hide evaders in a French forest rather than relaying them into Spain via their own successful Comet Line? Neave had full confidence in de Blommaert being able to convince the Comet leaders of the logic of his new plan. If that didn't work, he had given de Blommaert a significant sum of money – 2 million French francs – to make them see sense.

On 9 April 1944, de Blommaert and Ancia departed

from RAF Tempsford in Bedfordshire to be parachuted into France. Neave met them before they departed and was impressed by their calm and poise. De Blommaert was well aware of the great risk he was taking. He had narrowly avoided capture only a month before and knew that if he was taken prisoner this time it would inevitably result in torture and execution. Neave, however, was convinced the brave Belgian would complete his task successfully. 'Somehow, I felt certain that he would survive and that we should meet again,' Neave wrote. 'For after the invasion, I planned to lead the expedition to liberate the party in the Forêt de Fréteval myself.'[85]

After landing near Issoudun in France in the middle of the night, during which de Blommaert's parachute became tangled in overhead electric cables, the two of them made their way to Paris, where they arrived on 11 April. Here they discovered what was left of the Comet Line. Many of its Paris-based operatives had been arrested and the Line was in tatters and only in the south, under the stewardship of Madame de Greef,* was it still operational. It was imperative that the camp at Fréteval be prepared and that

---

* Madame de Greef was Elvire de Greef, the aunt of Andrée de Jongh and known as 'Tante Go' after her dog 'Go Go'. A slight, round-faced woman from Brussels, she had tried to escape to Britain in 1940 but was unable to do so. She moved with her husband and two children to live in the small village of Anglet in the shadow of the Pyrenees on the French–Spanish border. A crucial cog in the Comet Line, she was the principal co-ordinator and would make all the arrangements for the evaders arriving in St. Jean de Luz and hide them before they crossed into Spain. Knowing all the agents and smugglers in the area, she was able to obtain food and supplies as well as having a hold over the German officers by threatening to reveal their own supply of black market goods. Her husband, Fernand de Greef, worked for the German *Kommandantur* in Anglet as an official interpreter. As such he could access official stamps, blank identity cards and passes that he passed onto his wife to use. They operated from June 1941 until August 1944 without detection, and it is estimated that 360 Allied evaders passed through their hands on the way to Spain. After the war, Madame de Greef received the George Medal from Britain. She died in Brussels in 1991 aged 94.

evaders be moved there before all in Comet were betrayed. De Blommaert headed for Cloyes with an ever-growing sense of urgency, but before he left he met Philippe d'Albert Lake, a trusted and loyal member of Comet and one member yet to be discovered. Together they put in place a system of guides to transport the Allied evaders by train from Paris to Châteaudun, the nearest station to Fréteval.

Arriving in Cloyes, de Blommaert reported back to Neave in London that his contacts with the Resistance were 'of the greatest value'. Neave was thrilled to hear this and that the local farmers, bakers and tradesmen were all willing to assist and supply food on the black market for the evaders. De Blommaert also managed to convince the local Resistance that they should cease, with immediate effect, any acts of sabotage or subversion again the Germans stationed in Cloyes or near the forest. The aim was to keep the Germans out of the forest, possibly hunting the Resistance, and to ensure that following the D-Day invasion the retreating Germans would make for the Seine, leaving the forest in a no-man's land and easier to liberate.

With de Blommaert in position at Cloyes and Ancia working on a prospective camp in the Ardennes, Neave put into play his next piece of the operational jigsaw. Boussa had been part of the original group of Belgians working at 22 Pelham Crescent in London in early 1944, making preparations for Operation Marathon. He was in his forties and had had a noble flying career that included winning the Distinguished Flying Cross during the Battle of Britain following his escape to England from his native occupied

Belgium. He had the codename Belgrave and Neave described him as 'spare, energetic and amusing'.[86]

In May 1944, Boussa and his wireless operator Francois Toussaint landed in the north of Spain after crossing from Britain by boat and made their way into France. It was a difficult journey. From Spain the two of them had to cross the Pyrenees, meet up with the Comet Line in the Basque town of St Jean de Luz and then head north to Paris. But before he left Britain, Boussa had contacted the departmental head of the Resistance of Eure-et-Loir, Maurice Clavel, a twenty-three-year-old activist from Frontignan in southern France. Clavel had only just taken command of the Resistance in the Eure-et-Loir region and, unsure how he could help Boussa in his request to hide Allied airmen and evaders in Fréteval, took the advice of two colleagues who, in turn, pointed him in the direction of an ex-gendarme, Omer Jubault.

Jubault had worked in Cloyes for eight years and knew the area and the people inside out. He had also been a member of the Resistance and had actively taken part in clandestine operations against the occupying Germans in the area. However, he had been discovered and was facing imminent arrest by the Germans. Tipped off by his chief, who warned him that the Gestapo were closing in on him, Jubault disappeared on 10 January 1944 and went into hiding. Hunted as both a deserter and member of the Resistance, Jubault hid for months by changing his hiding place daily and relying only on the help of other patriotic Resistance members he knew he could trust.

Tracking down Jubault, Clavel informed him of Boussa's request and Neave's proposed plans. Jubault was fascinated with the proposal and keen to help in any way. He even saw the hiding of airmen as more important than his usual harassment of the occupying forces and, as chance would have it, he had somehow predicted the necessity to hide men in the forest as part of his actions with the Resistance. 'Foreseeing the operations which my group would be called upon to do at the time of the Liberation, I had set up different sites in the woods, having sources of drinking water, hiding places for arms, etc.,' Jubault recalled in a 1966 interview.

'In the Forest of Fréteval the Germans had set up small munition depots over several miles in the undergrowth bordering the forest paths, amounting in all to one or two lorry loads. In order to keep watch and to supplement guard posts installed in two forest huts, patrols covered the forest paths day and night. In addition, every so often, beats were organised in the forest by the officers of the Field Command at Vendôme for hunting big game. However, in the depths of the thick undergrowth where the enemy sentries did not venture, it was possible to hide the airmen without the protection of arms, so long as one essential was respected: to make as little noise as possible. The presence of the German troops kept away the curious. The site seemed just right.'[87]

By 18 May, Boussa and Toussaint had reached France and had met up with Clavel. Together they took the train to Châteaudun, a long and dangerous trip due to the fact the train was frequently attacked and bombed by Allied aircraft. Eventually, at 2 pm, some three hours late, the train arrived at Châteaudun. Waiting discreetly for them at the station with bicycles were Jubault and three other members of the Resistance: Maurice Serein, Lucien Bezault and Robert Poupard. Trying to avoid attention, the group began cycling in the direction of Forêt de Fréteval, 10 miles away.

A stop had been planned for them all at a small restaurant in the woods of Montigny-le-Gannelon where they would be fed. As the sun dropped, the group went on their way again and eventually arrived at the home of the local gamekeeper, Monsieur Hallouin. It was a small lodge on the edge of the forest at a place called Bellande, and was ideally hidden behind a little wood and concealed by a ring of trees from the nearby road on which German military transport was passing at all hours. It would be the perfect place to shelter a secret agent and Boussa needed no second invitation.

Jubault took the party into the woods and showed them the intended site. It was in a clumpy part of the forest, hidden behind thick foliage and with a spring of natural water just a hundred yards from the centre of the proposed camp. The Allies accepted it on the spot. De Blommaert had already scoured the area around Cloyes and found the ideal place for a dropping zone near Fréteval where supplies of food and arms could be parachuted in and a farm nearby, run by the Fouchard family, which would be the ideal place to store things, as well as being a slaughterhouse for animals to provide fresh meat.

With everything seemingly in order, Boussa went back

to Hallouin's lodge. Toussaint, his radio operator, stayed 10 miles away at the home of Dr Chaveau for reasons of basic security, and any necessary liaison between Boussa and Toussaint was conducted by Jubault's two children, Ginette and Jean, who were still at school. All the evaders would wear civilian clothes, supplied by their helpers, though getting such clothes proved difficult as Jubault later recalled. 'From the moment a patriot took in an Allied aviator, the first job was to get rid of his military uniform and dress him in civilian clothes, a fairly complicated job at that time. It was very difficult to get clothing. It was only given with tokens. The patriot was therefore obliged to dress his protégé himself. And because the aviator and his rescuer were often of very different sizes, it was not unusual to see a big chap wearing a pair of pants ending mid-calf with jacket sleeves ending at the elbow.

'The problem of shoes was even more difficult. Some aviators were wearing boots that it was necessary to take off immediately in order to avoid detection. Others who had walked long distances were wearing very worn-out shoes. In order to solve this difficulty, Daniel Lance, the tanner at Vendôme, secretly provided the necessary leather to a shoe-maker at d'Amboise. The finished shoes were distributed to the aviators as quickly as possible.'

Back in London, Neave had received radio communication confirming that Operation Sherwood was ready to go into action. There wasn't a moment to lose. It was time to bring the first evaders down from Paris and prepare them for life in the Forêt de Fréteval.

CHAPTER 11

THE WAIT

Neave was all too aware that the task facing everyone, particularly de Blommaert and Boussa, was an immense challenge. Transporting the evaders from Paris to Châteaudun and then into the forest was going to be perilous enough, but keeping up to five hundred men hidden under the noses of the Germans would test them to their limits. 'Success for the "Sherwood" plan depended', wrote Neave, 'on the personal leadership of de Blommaert and Boussa. Their principal problem would be to keep order in the forest and prevent the men, through impatience or claustrophobia, from making attempts to escape on their own.'[88]

For the evaders themselves, predominantly airmen, life on the run in France and Belgium had already proved a draining and at times demoralizing undertaking: the constant stress of imminent capture, the exhaustion of sleeping rough or in makeshift beds provided by strangers, the threat of betrayal and never knowing who to really trust, the uncertainty of their short-term future, their feeling of ineffectualness towards the war effort, being a stranger in a strange land and, perhaps most importantly, the lack of communication with friends and family affected them all deeply.

There were also the emotions of the Resistance families to consider; they were looking after foreign airmen, escaped strangers frequently unable to speak French, falling by chance into their hands and on their own with the least notion of the Resistance network. And all the time the fear of betrayal or discovery hung over them too from the threat of turncoat neighbours or agents working in towns and villages throughout France. Nobody was secure.

The evaders felt alone, distant and impotent. Abandoned too. But nothing could have been further from the truth. Neave and his dedicated team were seeing to that. Not that any of the downed fliers were aware of the efforts underway on their behalf.

Second Lieutenant Nelson Campbell, of the USAAF 365 Bomb Squadron, had been shot down over Belgium on 30 December 1943 and survived a crash-landing with his pilot and co-pilot. 'We were taken in that evening by a man and wife in their fifties. A priest and two other men came to see us. Early the next morning we walked to another farmhouse about six kilometres away. Then a butcher took us to his house. The pilot and co-pilot stayed with him. I stayed with Marcel Grimée and his mother; the family seemed to own a marble factory. I was there about ten days,' recalled Campbell.

A taxi collected them ten days later and they were moved to a deserted house in Chimay where an English-speaking school teacher looked after them. 'A young chap hiding out from the Germans was there. I believe he came from Luxembourg. I also met a Dutch flier named Joe, slim, tall, dark-haired, who seemed to take dope,' said Campbell. Before long Campbell was moved to Brussels, given forged identity papers and hidden in a room. But shortly after arriving in Brussels he was suddenly moved to another hideout 5 kilometres outside the city. The reason for his move was a chilling one: the Resistance had been penetrated. 'Just after we reached Brussels the chief of the group was caught in his office. We were also told that a German had gone through posing as a P-47 pilot. He had gone down the Line into France, but as I understood it he had not passed beyond Paris. The German turned in the men accompanying him and all the guides who had helped. For this reason, the Lines were out, and we were delayed,' Campell added.

Another airman hiding out was Second Lieutenant Donald Lewis of the USAAF 363 Fighter Group. He had been injured after parachuting out of his damaged aircraft and had been hidden in a house in Dampierre to the west of Paris. 'A member of the Resistance movement in Nonancourt came to see me. He sent for a doctor who refused to treat me. Next day, however, another doctor came to get me in an ambulance and took me to a hospital where I was kept in a small back room which seemed to be designed for such a purpose as it was well separated from the rest of the hospital, and provided a means of escape directly into the fields behind the hospital in the event of a search,' recalled Lewis. 'The only people in the hospital who knew of my presence there were two doctors and the pharmacist, all of whom treated me with great kindness and skill.

'Someone was detailed to stay with me twenty-four hours a day to keep me company and to help me get away if necessary, as the Gestapo was still searching for me in the neighbourhood. SS troops used the same hospital and were in it at the same time as I was. After I had been there a week it was reported that there was to be a search of the hospital, so I was taken to the house of some other helpers nearby.' Campbell stayed there three weeks before moving to a farmhouse nearby for a month and then finally to a home back in Dampierre belonging to the Lamoureux family where he recuperated, but always cautiously glancing over his shoulder with the constant threat of the Gestapo discovering him – and his helpers – at any moment.

Another downed airman was Jonathan 'Jack' Pearson III of the USAAF 95th Bomb Group, who had parachuted into France with Thomas Yankus after their B-17 Flying Fortress had been shot down on 3 March 1944, 30 kilometres north-west of St Quentin. Yankus discovered Pearson unconscious in the snow and revived him. For three days they hid in woods and slept in the snow before venturing out owing to starvation. He explained:

THE WAIT

We crept out of the woods and, screened by a gully, crept toward a road we could see in the distance. Along the road were a few stone houses with large fenced-in yards behind them. Slowly, we advanced on one where we could see chickens feeding. I think we hoped to find eggs or steal a chicken.

While we were plotting and watching, a woman came out to feed the birds and my companion persuaded me to call her since I spoke some French. She signalled us to climb the fence and come quickly to the back door. Inside, she and her husband examined us and interrogated us. They were very worried lest someone had seen us, and made it clear that we could not stay there. Eventually they provided us with some civilian clothing, a bottle of wine, some bread and hard-boiled eggs. We put the clothing over our heated flying suits and were wise enough to keep our army boots. With this we were taken to the front door and pushed out when it was clear that nobody was on the road. From here we set out for Paris and walked through St Quentin, Noyon and Compiègne, sleeping in haystacks and eating frozen potatoes, which dropped off the rear of a wagon.

Geno di Betta, an American pilot, had been on the run in France for even longer, since 11 February 1944. Taking off from Bedfordshire on his sixteenth mission, he was at the controls of his B-17 heavy bomber as it crossed the English Channel and headed into France en route to Saarbrücken. Shortly after midnight his plane was hit by flak in the wings and tail, and began leaking fuel. Di Betta made a desperate attempt to fly the plane back to England but as it was limping over France it came under further attack from German night-fighters. With one of his men killed in the gun turret, di Betta gave the order to bail out over Oise. During their descent and landing, the remaining crew members became separated and di Betta found himself alone in a field near the French village of Catillon, close to the Belgian border. He was also wounded in one hand.

From nowhere, an escaped Russian worker who was hiding in the fields came up to help di Betta, while other villagers helped him bury his parachute and flight equipment. He was rushed to a nearby farm and hidden in a hen house. Unable to speak French, di Betta was relieved to find the villagers brought him a doctor who spoke English and was able to take him to a café in St Just-en-Chausse. Here, di Betta faced a severe interrogation at the hands of Georges Jauneau, the local Resistance chief. Satisfied that di Betta was who he said he was, Jauneau took him to the house of Pierre Coulin in Bulles where di Betta was reunited with his co-pilot, Earl Wolf.

The following day the two airmen were taken to another café and hidden in the cellar awaiting collection by Dr Gaston Redaud. However, when Redaud arrived he found it full of German soldiers relaxing. Undeterred, he made his way into the kitchen and then down into the cellar. The café owner, a member of the Resistance, then guided them all to a secret door and they escaped across the garden to Redaud's car. He drove them to his house in Clermont where they stayed for a week before being moved on again to the home of the Fleury family where, incredibly, di Betta and Wolf were reunited with the rest of their crew whom they hadn't seen since bailing out. But their reunion was short-lived. After a couple of days they were separated into smaller groups and taken to different houses. They were given identity cards with their new French pseudonyms and certificates of residence.

While Wolf was one of sixteen men transported back to Dartmouth, England, on a high-speed motor gun boat on the night of 20 March 1944, di Betta was sent to stay at the house of Henri Lestienne in Vineuil-Saint-Firmin for six weeks and then on to another house in Neuilly-en-Thelle for a further three weeks. Finally, after being ferried to two more houses where he was concealed – such was the lot of the Allied evader – he finally arrived at the home of Henri Maigret in Argenteuil where he stayed for another five weeks before he was finally taken to Fréteval Forest. His relief at arriving there must have been overwhelming.

He had been on the run for almost four months, depending on the help of local Resistance members to keep him hidden, fed and watered. He never knew entirely whom he could trust, aware that with each relay to a new helper he could be walking straight into the hands of a double agent. Such a period of evasion was exhausting, full of tension and unpredictability. But finally he made it to Fréteval – one of the first evaders to do so.

Canadian Bill Brayley was, like Campbell, di Betta, Pearson and Lewis, also on the run in France. He had bailed out from his burning Halifax on 10 April 1944 and was ferried between families of the Resistance before arriving in Paris where he found himself sharing an apartment with Yankus, amongst others. It was at this large studio-type apartment in the Rue Vaneau, owned by Lake and his American wife, Virginia, that the young airmen were hidden away from the eyes and ears of the Germans. Here they rested while the husband and wife team organised their escape, having interrogated them to ensure they were genuine, and approve them for the camp.

Meanwhile, not far away, more Allied airmen were hiding in another helper's home, this time virtually in the shadow of the Eiffel Tower. In the sixth-floor apartment at 8 Rue de Montessuy of Madame René Melison, they were also awaiting the next stage of their journey. As ever, secrecy was vital otherwise the whole of the Paris organisation could be brought down, thereby having a catastrophic impact on the Sherwood plan. The Germans made regular house-checks in Paris and, just before the airmen arrived at Madame Melison's apartment, a visit from the police occurred. Nothing unusual was found and they left, but because her apartment was on the sixth floor and there was no elevator in the building they never visited her apartment again. Maybe the climb up six flights was too much? So, perhaps more by luck rather than management, no Allied airmen were discovered in Melison's apartment.

Elsewhere, Worrall, Hallett and dozens of other downed airmen were dodging the Germans in France, hiding out where they could, helped by the French Resistance and waiting for whatever would happen next. They had no idea of the plan to conceal them all together in a forest camp but, with D-Day now imminent, Neave instructed those controlling the Sherwood operation that the first airmen be taken to Châteaudun from Paris, and readied for transport to the forest. It was 20 May 1944 and thirty Allied airmen made the journey, including Joseph Peloquin, an American of French-Canadian descent from Biddeford, Maine.

'My plane was shot down at Patay, about nineteen kilometres north-west of Orleans,' he said. German Me 109 fighter planes had attacked his aircraft as it targeted the Marshalling Yards at Mulhouse. The ten-man crew – from Missouri, Pennsylvania, Oregan, Kansas, New Jersey, New York and Maine – bailed out after their number one engine caught fire and the plane began to go down. 'When I jumped out,' Peloquin added, 'I counted to about ten – enough to clear the plane. We were at about 15,000 feet at that time, and I pulled my ripcord but nothing happened. No 'chute. I was falling free at 120 mph and I tugged and pulled at the flaps on my 'chute, and finally pulled out a little of the silk or nylon. As I kept pulling, the pilot 'chute came out and it released the main 'chute. All of this took so long that when it finally blossomed out, I was just 300 feet from the ground! This is one of the reasons the Germans didn't spot me coming down.'

Landing heavily, with Germans searching the vicinity, Peloquin injured his left heel. It wasn't his only injury. 'I too had been hit by the shrapnel from that exploding shell that hit Puksta [rear gunner Edwin A. Puksta, who survived his injuries and was taken prisoner]. I had one in my arm above the elbow and several small ones in my face and another one in my neck, which I still have there. It just missed my jugular vein.'[89] Despite his injuries, Peloquin managed to get some distance away from the Germans before approaching a French woman who found a doctor to treat his wounds. Shortly afterwards a local gendarme arranged for him to be taken to Orleans by members of the Resistance. He was placed in the southern part of the town where he stayed with Mlle Morlette, whose son-in-law had contacts with the Resistance in Paris, where Peloquin was sent next. While in Paris, Peloquin expected to be constantly hidden, concealed within some attic or secret room, deprived of light, fresh air and with only meagre rations to eat. However, one day he received an unexpected surprise when Annie, one of the Resistance members, 'took us out one bright Sunday for a tour of Paris, including a visit to Les Invalides and the tomb of Napoleon. The tomb was a favourite with German soldiers and we were surrounded by them as we peered down at the crypt. Our guides showed no concern whatsoever, so neither did we.' Then, after a week, 'members of the Paris organisation came and took me to Châteaudun where I met de Blommaert, the camp manager'.

None of the first thirty airmen were taken directly to the forest at Fréteval. Instead, they were hidden in neighbouring villages. Peloquin was sent with eight other evaders to stay with the Barbier family to the south of Châteaudun. He – and the other twenty-nine airmen – didn't know it, but they would have to wait until the D-Day invasion before they could be taken to the forest. And that was two weeks away.

CHAPTER 12

THE GREEN LIGHT

'Soldiers, Sailors and Airmen of the Allied Expeditionary Force! You are about to embark upon the Great Crusade, toward which we have striven these many months. The eyes of the world are upon you. The hopes and prayers of liberty-loving people everywhere march with you. […] Your task will not be an easy one. Your enemy is well trained, well equipped and battle-hardened. He will fight savagely. But this is the year 1944! […] The tide has turned! The free men of the world are marching together to victory! I have full confidence in your courage, devotion to duty and skill in battle. We will accept nothing less than full victory! Good luck! And let us all beseech the blessing of Almighty God upon this great and noble undertaking.' So decreed the Supreme

Allied Commander, General Dwight D. Eisenhower, on 6 June 1944: D-Day.*

The train of events that would lead to D-Day began in 1941 following the Japanese attack on Pearl Harbor on the morning of 7 December. This brought the USA directly into World War II with US president Franklin Roosevelt announcing the country was at war with Japan on 8 December. Three days later Italian dictator Benito Mussolini proclaimed Italy was at war with the USA, pledging that the 'powers of the pact of steel', a bilateral alliance between Germany and Italy, were determined to win. Shortly after Mussolini's statement, Hitler announced from the Reichstag in Berlin that, although he had tried to avoid direct conflict with the USA, under the terms of the Tripartite Agreement signed on 27 September 1940 Germany was obliged to join with Italy to defend its ally, Japan.† 'After victory has been achieved,' Hitler proclaimed, 'Germany, Italy and Japan will continue in closest co-operation with a view to establishing a new and just order.'

On 22 December 1941, Churchill arrived in Washington, DC, to meet President Roosevelt. Following Pearl Harbor, Churchill had sent a message to Roosevelt saying, 'Now that we are, as you say, "in the same boat", would it not be

---

* 'The D-Day moniker wasn't invented for the Allied invasion. The same name had been attached to the date of every planned offensive of World War II. It was first coined during World War I, at the US attack at the Battle of Saint-Mihiel, in France, in 1918. The D was short for *day*. The expression literally meant "day-day" and signified the day of an attack. By the end of World War II, however, the phrase had become synonymous with a single date: June 6, 1944.' 'The Longest Day', Douglas Brinkley (*Time*, 20 May 2014)

† The Tripartite Act of September 1940 stated that Japan would recognise and respect the 'leadership' of Germany and Italy in the 'establishment of a new order' in Europe, and that Germany and Italy would recognise and respect the 'leadership' of Japan in the 'establishment of a new order' in 'Greater East Asia'.

wise for us to have another conference. We could review the whole war plan in the light of reality and new facts.' (It seems strange now, given America's position as the number one global superpower in terms of military might, that in June 1939 the US Army consisted of only 180,000 men, smaller than Portugal's army, thanks to the reluctance in peacetime of the 'isolationist' Congress to authorize military expenditure and the US Army was ranked nineteenth in the world in terms of strength.)[90]

Any link between the USA and the Britain would not only benefit beleaguered Britain but would also allow Roosevelt to strengthen ties between the two. Britain was 'The one nation whose combined military, political and economic strength might serve as a bulwark against a possible Axis aggression in the Western Hemisphere,' wrote David Woolner. Moreover, 'It is hard for most Americans to imagine a time when we might look to Great Britain and the Royal Navy as America's first line of defence; yet on the eve of the Second World War until well into the early 1940s, Great Britain's combined military strength exceeded that of the United States. FDR was well aware of this. He also understood that it would take time for the United States to catch up with her potential allies and adversaries. Hence one of the fastest and most efficient means for him to bolster America's security was to strengthen the ties between Great Britain and the United States.'[91]

Churchill and Roosevelt had met once before, in August 1941, off Newfoundland where they had signed the Atlantic Charter, a declaration of common principles that would follow 'the final destruction of Nazi tyranny'. Now, in December, having sailed to the USA on the Royal Navy's newest battleship, HMS *Duke of York*, Churchill and Roosevelt met for a three-week conference codenamed Arcadia. During the talks, Churchill proposed an Anglo-American invasion of French North Africa and the two men agreed that the USAAF should also join the RAF Bomber Command in its offensive against targets in Nazi-occupied Europe, as well as a naval blockade of Germany. They also concurred on generous assistance to the Soviet Union in its battle against the Nazis on the Eastern Front. At midnight on New Year's Eve, following the conclusion of the talks, Churchill toasted reporters with 'Here's to 1942. Here's to a long year of toil – a year of struggle and peril, and a long step forward towards victory.'

By April 1942, US troops and military infrastructure had started to arrive in Britain as part of Operation Bolero, the codename for the transfer of fighting men and equipment from the USA and Canada across the Atlantic in preparation for a cross-Channel invasion. Discussions about the invasion of Europe had already begun, and it was agreed that only a direct assault on Hitler's empire could result in victory. In fact, the Americans had already been putting pressure on Britain to launch an invasion on Europe. Before Bolero began in earnest, General Marshall, the US Chief of Staff and confidant of President Roosevelt, had travelled to the UK with two invasion plans.

The first was for a full-scale invasion by 48 Allied divisions landing in France supported by 5,800 combat aircraft. It was codenamed Operation Roundup and would take place before April 1943. The second was Operation Sledgehammer, to be undertaken almost entirely by the British, supported by only two or three American divisions in seizing Cherbourg and some of the Cotentin peninsula. Once seized, the British would have to hold it through the winter until, bolstered by more Allied troops, they would mount a breakout in the spring of 1943. The American idea for Sledgehammer was backed up by a veiled threat to the British that if it wasn't carried out the Americans would instead direct their war effort against Japan.

It was nothing short of blackmail, but the proposed operation was absolute folly. The port of Cherbourg had had its defences heavily strengthened by the Germans. In addition, they had up to thirty divisions in the surrounding area, many of them armoured providing formidable back-up. The British would only be able to put ashore six divisions, making it all but impossible to capture the port. The potential for catastrophe was huge. The British stood their ground, rebuffed the Operation Sledgehammer plan and, instead, gave their tentative support to Roundup, which would take place in the spring or summer of 1943. As a consequence, the Americans reluctantly abandoned Sledgehammer on 24 July 1942 to concentrate on the North African landings in November, codenamed Operation Torch, followed by Roundup the following year. But General Marshall wasn't impressed with the British attitude: 'Even though we must reluctantly agree to no Sledgehammer in 1942, I still think we should press forward vigorously for the 1943 enterprise. I see nothing in the message from England to indicate any luke-warmness on their part for the 1943 enterprise. I am somewhat disturbed about their readiness to give up in 1942. Will they also give up in 1943?'[92]

For the European invasion, the Americans wanted to attack the Pas de Calais, the shortest distance across the Channel and, therefore, the most obvious place for a seaborne assault. However, being a natural target meant it was also very heavily defended by the Germans. The British, in contrast, favoured landing on the Normandy coast. It was a less obvious target, didn't have such extensive defences and was perfectly placed for operations from Plymouth, Southampton and Portsmouth.

As Operation Bolero continued and British ports became clogged with shipping of every description, with the countryside beginning to resemble one massive ammunitions dump and the towns and villages in southern England becoming awash with American soldiers, sailors and airmen, the planning for D-Day continued at the highest level and, to put the Germans off the scent, elaborate deception plans were put into operation.

The plan was to launch an invasion in 1943, but the disastrous Allied raid on the French coastal town of Dieppe on 19 August 1942, where 4,131 troops of the 6,000-strong Canadian and British force were killed, wounded or captured in just six hours, and 106 RAF aircraft were lost along with the destroyer HMS *Berkeley*,[93] highlighted just how difficult a seaborne assault across the English Channel would be. Nevertheless, planning for Operation Roundup continued. This proposal would see 18 British and 30 American divisions hitting a series of landing zones between Calais and Le Havre with 5,800 combat aircraft supporting them from the sky. This would then pave the way for more Allied troops to be parachuted in.

But by the time of the Casablanca Conference in January 1943, held at the Anfa Hotel and attended by Roosevelt and Churchill – as well as by General de Gaulle and Henri Giraud representing the Free French forces – it was agreed that a large-scale invasion of Europe via a cross-channel operation would be impracticable before the spring of 1944.

On 7 December 1943, General Dwight D. Eisenhower was promoted to overall commander of what was now codenamed Operation Overlord. The British suggestion of landing on the Normandy beaches had been approved and across southern Britain, under a veil of complete secrecy, preparation and planning for the invasion gathered pace. In early 1944, Eisenhower joined the Supreme Headquarters Allied Expeditionary Force (SHAEF) in London to make sure the final pieces of the jigsaw were falling into place. By June 1944, over 1.5 million US military personnel had arrived in the UK as a result of Bolero, with over a quarter of a million Canadian, French, Polish, Dutch, Belgian and Czech troops swelling the numbers.

Training was intense and undertaken at all levels of command, but from the beginning it all too plainly revealed problems with communication, lack of mission comprehension and poor crisis management abilities. It was obvious that a general sense of chaos overshadowed preparations. Nowhere was this more evident than in the training disaster at Slapton Sands, Devon, in the early hours of 28 April 1944. Exercise Tiger – a dummy invasion involving thousands of men, a flotilla of landing craft, amphibious trucks, jeeps and live ammunition – went tragically wrong as a group of German E-boats, alerted by heavy radio traffic in Lyme Bay, intercepted the three-mile-long convoy of vessels. Three of the Allied ships were hit, and it is believed that at least 749 American soldiers died – more deaths than during the actual D-Day landing on Utah Beach less than two months later.

'In comparison to the E-boat attack, Utah Beach was a walk in the park,' said Exercise Tiger and D-Day survivor Steve Sadlon sixty-five years later.[94] So sensitive was the tragedy, and so worried were the authorities that it would affect morale in the run-up to D-Day, that those who had witnessed events were sworn to secrecy and, despite rumours amongst elderly villagers in South Devon of mass graves, the tragedy wasn't revealed until forty years later.

While secrecy was paramount, the Allies did decide to leak some information. This was part of a monumental deception plan codenamed Operation Bodyguard, in which they continually drip-fed the Germans misinformation. As Churchill told Roosevelt, 'Truth is so precious that she must often be attended by a bodyguard of lies.' The most imaginative of minds were employed to create the most deceptive of strategies. One went under the codename of Operation Fortitude North, and involved twenty-eight middle-aged British officers and their radio officers being sent to a castle in Scotland to suggest, via a low-level coded cipher that the Germans could easily crack, that the British Fourth Army, a fictitious 250,000-man force based in Edinburgh, was preparing to invade Norway. 'It was known that the Germans in Norway were taking an active interest in what we were doing,' recalled Captain Joe Brown, a young officer of the 7th/9th Royal Scots who was involved in the deception. 'We knew they could intercept our radio signals during training, and our unwitting occasional breaches of radio discipline provided them with varying intelligence that we were being trained to liberate Norway.'

Elsewhere, dummy tanks, Spitfires, landing craft and even airfields were created in the south of England to give the Germans the impression that the Allies would invade the Pas de Calais in mid-July, and this was supported by the actions of Juan Pujol García ('Garbo'), a Spanish double agent who passed false information to the Germans. Even struggling actor M.E. Clifton James from Perth, Australia, was brought in to impersonate General Montgomery and make public appearances in Gibraltar and North Africa to suggest the invasion might take place via the Mediterranean.*

---

*   Clifton James' role in playing Montgomery was, perhaps, the biggest role he ever had and also the most detrimental to his acting career as the *Carnarvon Northern Times* in Western Australia revealed on 4 April 1947: 'Man who pulled one of the biggest bluffs of the war, doubling for Field-Marshal Montgomery, lined up for the dole at the London Labor Exchange recently. He is Edward Clifton James, who, when a lieutenant in the Royal Army Pay Corps, doubled for Montgomery in the Mediterranean on the eve of D-Day, fooling the Germans about the date. Clifton James received the dole because he needed support for his wife and 2 children. Twenty years ago, he started acting with Fred Karno, but since he was demobbed last June has only had 3 days work. He explained that managers said his presence on the stage would be disturbing because people would go to the theatre only to see Montys double. Clifton James said: "No actor ever got more publicity than I did. Managers and others rushed to greet me, set me on a pedestal for all to see – but none of them thought of offering me a job."'

With troops, arms and infrastructure gathered and ready to go, and the deceptions in full swing, the Allies decided to invade on 1 May 1944. But this was almost immediately cancelled when they discovered that they were short of 271 LSTs, the ships built to support amphibious operations by carrying tanks, vehicles, cargo and landing troops directly onshore without using docks or piers. This left an invasion window of just a few days in either the first or third week of June, dates which were based on tides, the moon, training and the availability of equipment.

For the invasion to have the best chance of success, Eisenhower needed a full moon, light winds and a low tide (this was crucial if the soldiers were to see, avoid and disarm the mined obstacles that the Germans had placed in the surf just off the Normandy beaches). For a full moon and low tide, the ideal invasion dates were 5–7 June. If the invasion didn't happen on those dates then Eisenhower would have to wait until 19 or 20 June, but on those dates he would only have a low tide. There would be no full moon. And then the weather had to be good.

Eisenhower decided to set the new date for D-Day to 5 June. But with 6,000 ships ready to go, the invasion force in position and some vessels having even started the crossing (the first ships for the invasion had actually left Scotland on 28 May), disaster loomed. 'Into the middle of this armada came the chief meteorologist, Group Captain James Martin Stagg, a terse Scot with a long, thin, pale face, closely cropped hair and a severe moustache to report that his three teams of meteorologists – conferring and arguing by telephone – had grudgingly reached agreement. The weather for 5 June would be bad, very bad. Winds in the channel were likely to be force 5 on the Beaufort Scale, a stiff breeze, not yet a gale, but enough to set up a swell that would trouble ordinary ships never mind the landing craft. Worse, the sky would be overcast, and the cloud base at only 500 feet, making the launching of paratroopers impossible, rendering precision bombing of the defences out of the question and making it too difficult for naval gunners to judge the accuracy of their salvos.'[95]

Eisenhower was forced to postpone D-Day by twenty-four hours. Then, early in the morning of 6 June, with the weather finally good enough to commence, he uttered the three words that set D-Day in motion: 'Okay, let's go.' The invasion was under way.*

By the end of the day Hitler's seawall had been breached and the Allies were dug in all across the front. Ahead they faced seven weeks of fierce fighting; only then would the Normandy campaign be won. But the Allies had achieved what they set out to do, establish a foothold on the Continent and they were inching their way towards the downed Allied airmen hiding in France.

---

* An interesting postscript to the launching of D-Day on 6 June is that, although the weather had improved, the Germans thought it was still bad enough to prevent an invasion as Logan revealed in *Air: The Restless Shaper*. 'The Germans believed that the weather was too bad for the Allies to invade. This was not the fault of poor forecasting. Group Captain Heinz Lettau—later a revered professor of meteorology at the University of Wisconsin—saw the same succession of fronts as did the Allied forecasters. He may or may not have noted the marginal improvement of the weather on the 6th. Even had he seen this, however, his orders were clear. The High Command had decided that an invasion was not possible if there was a risk of the winds reaching force 4 or higher. (The Germans had put off their own planned invasion of Britain, Operation Sea Lion, in 1940, in part because they could never get what they felt was a calm-enough sea for the troops to cross.) Lettau was confident—and right—that there would be a force 4 wind on June 5, 6, and 7. Ergo, there could be no invasion. What the Germans failed to find out was that the Allies thought force 4 was just fine.'

THE HIDDEN ARMY

Now Neave put the next part of Operation Sherwood into action and began moving some of the evaders to his secret camp deep within the forest at Fréteval.

CHAPTER 13

THE FIRST MEN IN

In the two weeks leading up to D-Day, thirty downed Allied airmen had been hidden in the neighbouring villages around Fréteval after they had disembarked from their train at Châteaudun and been escorted by courageous Resistance members, led by Daniel Cogneau, to their hiding places with other Resistance families in houses nearby. Amongst them was Flight Lieutenant 'Pete' Berry.

From Paris, where he had been concealed in a flat close to the Eiffel Tower, he was taken by his guide Anne to a railway station in the French capital where he met up with Tom Yankus and Jim Pearson III and their guide, Germaine. Here they boarded a morning train to Châteaudun. At this point they still had no idea what the evasion plan for them consisted of. They attempted to blend in and make themselves as anonymous as they could. No words were exchanged, no furtive glances at the SS troops on the train, no hands in pockets and no chewing gum. For security, their guides sat elsewhere but always kept them in sight. If the evaders were caught it was vital the guides get away. Similarly, if the guides were apprehended then the evaders must remain at large.

As they left Paris everything was going smoothly, but only 10 miles outside their train came to a shuddering stop at Choisy-le-Roi. The evaders couldn't help but look around nervously as the SS troops onboard became alert and started moving through the carriages to the exits. The female guides looked anxiously back towards their 'packages', everyone wondering what was going on. Moments later they were all ordered off. Barely understanding the orders from the SS, the evaders followed everyone else in clambering out and they mingled with the other passengers on the sidings, plotting an escape route should events take a turn for the worst.

As tensions rose news filtered down the line that the track ahead had been bombed and the train could go no farther. So they all began the 10-mile trek along the banks of the River Seine to the next station at Juvisy-sur-Orge where another train was waiting. But the danger wasn't over. Finally arriving in Châteaudun, the evaders and their guides were shocked to find the station full of German soldiers. Most were waiting to catch a train, others on the lookout for anything or anyone suspicious.

Once again the evaders had to sink into the shadows as Germaine set about trying to find their contact, Jubault – the man with the bicycle, that was all they knew – who would lead them on the next leg of the journey. But so congested was the station that Germaine couldn't find him. It was an incredibly tense and perilous moment for all concerned, and she had to avoid appearing flustered and anxious to ensure she didn't attract attention. And for Jubault himself, already being sought by the Gestapo and the secret police for being part of the Resistance, and by the French police for desertion, every minute spent amongst crowds where Germans soldiers and agents gathered meant an increased likelihood of him being discovered.

Finally, after what seemed like an eternity, Germaine found Jubault who, with a subtle signal, ordered her and the evaders to follow him as he cycled off. At a safe distance from the railway station, he stopped cycling and pretended to pump up his tyre, letting them catch up. Ahead lay a 25-mile walk. The evaders were hungry, thirsty and weary but couldn't stop. For Berry the walk promised to be a painful one: he had removed his shoes at the station as his feet were covered in blisters, and now he had to complete the walk in stockinged feet. Despite this, Berry and the party reached the area around Fréteval in the evening.

Unbeknown to them, twenty-five other evaders were already there, concealed within the houses of families with Resistance connections. Berry was lodged at the home of Armand Guet, a farmer at Audrieres near Cloyes. Five other evaders were lodging in an isolated house with Pierre Van Bever in the village of Saint-Hilaire-sur-Yerre. Monsieur Doubouchage, a bricklayer at Rameau, was hiding five airmen, and two were lodged at the home of Madame

Chesneau at Chanteloup. Two more were hidden at the home of René Jacques and two at the home of the Station Master at Saint-Jean-Froidmentel, while the remaining airmen were being taken care of by Gustave Barbier, Madame Guerineau and Martinez Pedro in nearby Morée and Monsieur Fouchard, a farmer at Bellande.

Throughout these two weeks, Boussa took it upon himself to make daily visits to all of the thirty evaders scattered throughout the region. He needed to reassure himself that they were being well looked after, and that they were staying mentally and physically strong in readiness for the next leg of the evasion plan, not an easy task when rations were all they had to live on and exercise and exposure to the outside was at a minimum through necessity.

To visit each of these men was a huge personal risk to Boussa. The area was swarming with German soldiers and patrols, and the risk of betrayal by any of the French helpers who may have been a secret German agent was ever present. After all, one of the reasons Sherwood existed was because the Comet Line had been compromised. For all their best checks and due diligence, nobody could really be sure who to trust. If Boussa had been observed, tracked or followed, not only would he have led the Germans directly to the thirty airmen but he would have exposed crucial cogs within the French Resistance. Sherwood would collapse immediately and those helping – the many local families, Jubault and Hallouin – would have been deported to concentration camps, if they weren't executed on the spot. Just a couple of months earlier, on 30 March, thirty-one Resistance members in the region had been executed for helping the Allies and fourteen villagers from Vendôme had been sent to concentration camps for having sheltered the crew of an Allied aircraft.

The evaders also risked being shot: they were disguised in civilian clothing and, as such, no longer had the protection that a military uniform gave them. If they were discovered in civilian clothing the Germans could have them shot as spies or insurgents.

Aware of the risks he was taking by frequently using the same country roads to visit the evaders, Boussa appealed for help and, two days later, Jean de Blommaert arrived from Paris accompanied by Philippe d'Albert Lake. They took some of the pressure, and risk, off Boussa.

In the two weeks between the evaders arriving in the vicinity of Fréteval and the D-Day invasion at Normandy, the Resistance, particularly Jubault, had managed to procure a number of tarpaulins from local farmers that they used to construct basic tents to shelter the men in the camp. One of these tarpaulins had come all the way from Dunkirk, and all of them were concealed deep within the forest, out of sight of any passing Germans.

Boussa and the five airmen being hidden at the farm of Monsieur Fouchard now ventured into the forest to set up the camp. De Blommaert and Lake helped out, slinging the tarpaulins over branches and clearing an area of scrub, while Dr Dufour from Chartres, 30 miles to the north of Châteaudun, exploited the fact he could travel by car because of his profession to transport provisions to the camp, including food, utensils for cooking and tobacco. Jubault, had also been industrious in the previous weeks whilst on the run from the Germans, and had hidden basic provisions at sites within the forest for his own personal use should he need to hide there. He now gave them to the camp.

By the time D-Day arrived, they had pitched a number of tents and established the basic necessities for camp life, including plans for three sentries to be posted at points at the edge of the woods to keep watch. Then, on 6 June, with D-Day in full swing, news of the invasion filtered through and reached the evaders causing great excitement and hope. On the beaches at Normandy, Allied troops were storming ashore. In the skies above Europe, British and American troops were parachuting into France. And silently floating down were Horsa and CG-4 gliders – also known as Flying Coffins – to land troops and cement the advance on German positions. 'We heard of the invasion from local people. Then Jean [de Blommaert] arrived,' recalled Berry. 'He had been a Belgian officer before the war and had three years with the organisation. He is a fine man and understands the English temperament better than Lucien [Boussa] does.'

At this point few of the evaders knew what was being planned for them. Only the handful who had helped construct the tents had any idea but, being isolated from the others, couldn't pass on any information, rumours or gossip. During his visit to Berry on 6 June, de Blommaert finally revealed to him the plans for Operation Sherwood. He also had a specific request for Berry that took the Englishman by surprise: 'Jean told me about forming a new camp in the district for escapers and evaders, and that I was to be camp commander in charge of the internal working of the camp. He and Lucien would be our outside contacts; they would organise and supply the food for the camp, and bring in escapers and evaders.'

Berry had no experience of leadership within the RAF, he was simply a flight lieutenant, a junior rank above that of flying officer and below squadron leader. And he was a rear gunner to boot. Pre-war he had been a tobacconist in London, not an occupation that that would appear to provide foundations for military leadership. Perhaps the reason de Blommaert chose him was that the only other Englishman, Flight Sergeant Dennis Pepall, was a non-commissioned rank while the Canadian Brayley was a junior rank, as were the two Americans. It was a decision that proved to be unpopular later on, but for now Berry accepted the role and, on 7 June, after de Blommaert had provided him with a replacement pair of shoes, he made his first foray into Fréteval Forest to view the camp that awaited him and the other evaders. That evening, content with what he had seen and excited about commanding this bold evasion plan, Berry moved into the camp and slept the first night alone in the forest.

Meanwhile, back in Britain hundreds of aircraft were still taking off to support the D-Day invasion. One man taking to the skies was a twenty-three-year-old Canadian, Flying Officer Bill Vickerman from Sedgewick, Alberta. He had never heard of Fréteval but within days it would give him sanctuary, and within weeks over 150 Allied evaders would join him beneath the trees.

Vickerman had already been involved on an overnight mission on 6 June, flying alongside the other aircraft from 432 Squadron to bomb the railway yards at Coutances in north-western France. He was new to the air and his first bombing run had only taken place three weeks previously when his aircraft had been hit by armour-piercing ammunition from one of their own planes. Managing to make it home had given Vickerman a vivid insight into the dangers facing him and his crew.

Returning from the 6 June mission, as dawn broke the following day, they were given the news they least wanted to hear: they were to be sent out on another mission that night, this time bombing railway marshalling yards in a suburb of Paris. After a few hours sleep while their plane was prepared again, they were briefed and given a pre-flight meal before being ferried by bus to their waiting Halifax, nicknamed 'Pistol Packin' Mama'. Shortly afterwards, the aircraft lumbered down the runway at RAF East Moor in Yorkshire, picked up speed and climbed into the night sky. They headed south-west of the French town of Beauvais, a path taking them directly into the airspace of a large Luftwaffe airbase.

Just before midnight, one of the bombers in the group radioed in that German fighters had been spotted and before they knew it Vickerman's Halifax had a deadly Ju 88 on its tail. Seconds later, the fuel tanks of the Halifax were hit, and the Ju banked away for fear of being destroyed by the exploding bombs still in the bomb bay.

On fire and going down, Vickerman ordered his crew to bail out. Six of the seven crew made it. Rear gunner Sergeant Frederick Layton couldn't escape the burning aircraft; he was twenty years old.

The next thing Vickerman remembered was being shaken out of unconsciousness by nineteen-year-old Canadian Noe Beauchesne, his mid-upper gunner, and being surrounded by a smell of burning. Regaining his senses, he heard German voices close-by shouting through the darkness. He was helped to his feet by Beauchesne, the two of them hid in bushes nearby for what seemed like an eternity until they heard the noise of vehicles starting up and the German voices disappearing. Breaking cover, they began running and they were on the run all night until dawn broke. During daylight, they hid on the edge of a forest and then, when night fell, set off again.

Not knowing where they were or where they were going, they found themselves in a terrible predicament: one they had been trained for (up to a point) but one they had hoped would never befall them. To make matters worse, Vickerman's right arm had been burnt bailing out and a bad smell told him it was getting infected.

The following morning they spotted a farmer in a field and decided to approach him. They needed help – food, shelter and a doctor. The farmer took them back to his house and instructed his son to go into town to get the butcher. Vickerman got anxious. Were they going to amputate? As it happened, there was also a young chemist staying at the farm who spoke a bit of English; he cleaned and dressed his arm to avoid the need for any rudimentary butchery.

Later a car pulled up. They were instantly on edge; was it assistance or had they been betrayed? Fortunately, it was Monsieur Lejeune, the local butcher and a member of the Resistance. After many questions, Lejeune realised that the two downed airmen weren't German agents, and they were taken, concealed under blankets in the back of Lejeune's car, to the nearby village of Sérifontaine. Half an hour later they arrived at the butcher's shop where they were hidden and finally got some sleep. 'After forty-eight hours on the go we were a bit tired,' Beauchesne added. 'The butcher awoke us the next afternoon and, attesting to the underground's incredible efficiency, presented us with identification papers, complete with the picture supplied to us by the air force (part of their emergency kit). I now had a new name, a Norman name, because we were in the Normandy area. I was now Paul Louis Lemarche and we were also given some civilian clothes.'[96] Vickerman also had a new identity: Robert Ribault.

On 9 June, the two men were taken to the nearby town of Argenteuil where they were hidden on the outskirts in the house of a café owner, before being moved constantly between houses, one of which was owned by Madame Bredèche and her husband. Evaders couldn't stay in one place for long. They had to be moved to avoid any suspicion and threat of detection. It was a strategy that worked well for many evaders and their helpers, including Vickerman and Beauchesne. 'We remained there for a few days and then were taken back to Mme Bredèche for a day, but as it was not considered safe to remain any length of time in one place, it was arranged for us to stay for a few days with Mnsr Potevin, a butcher who had helped several American pilots. Mnsr Potevin introduced us to a Belgian woman, and it was arranged. She would take us to Paris by train,' Vickerman said.[97]

Paris was a dangerous place for an Allied evader. The Germans were scouring the streets and houses for the secret hiding places of downed airmen and those Resistance helpers hiding them. With the Allies establishing a foothold in Normandy following the invasion, the secret police and Gestapo were becoming ever more brutal and unpredictable throughout France. It was vital, therefore, that Beauchesne and Vickerman were conveyed out of Paris as quickly as possible. As it happened, they spent only one night in the city – 19 June. The following day, the Belgian woman took them both to the railway station and handed them over to a French girl who gave them two train tickets. She would also accompany them on the train. Their destination was Châteaudun. But they had no idea what awaited them.

Obeying the instructions to follow a few steps behind, be discreet and keep their heads down, they walked along the platform. They boarded the train, their French guide taking a seat some distance away, and settled into two empty seats in a compartment. Moments later, two German officers entered the compartment and sat opposite them, settling into a conversation and seeming to ignore the two 'civilians'. 'Oh, the thoughts that go through one's mind at a time like that,' Beauchesne remembered, years later. 'The train had gone about 10 kilometres beyond Paris when our guide got off and we duly followed,'[98] he added. They had arrived in a place called Étampes, a pretty town on the River Chalouette. But there was no time for sightseeing. What followed was five days of solid walking across fields and down back-roads as they were led by a series of different guides to Châteaudun, some seventy-five miles away. By the time they reached Châteaudun, Vickerman's feet were shredded but at least, here, he could rest. The two evaders were hidden overnight with a Resistance helper. In the morning, they would make the final 10-mile trek to their destination – Fréteval Forest.

But by the time Vickerman arrived, dozens of Allied evaders were already ensconced in the forest camp. With the Allies by now having landed on the beaches in Normandy and D-Day firmly underway, Neave's plan had swung into action. Sherwood was now in operation. After his first night alone in the forest camp, Berry was joined the following day by four American evaders along with Pepall and Brayley. Berry recalled declaring the camp officially open on 10 June 'with about ten of us. Then more escapers and evaders started arriving.'

From his hiding place with the Barbier family, Peloquin and the other eight airmen hiding there with him carefully made their way towards the forest. They still had no idea where they were going: they simply had to trust their guides.

Bundled into a van, they found themselves alongside other airmen and Peloquin was both surprised and delighted to find that one of them was his crew member, gunner Lawrence Richards, whom he hadn't seen since they all bailed out. The vehicle trundled along the country roads, the airmen in the back staying silent. At any moment a German patrol could stop them and, if their Resistance guides couldn't talk their way out of it, it would be everyman for himself, a less-than-appealing prospect for any Allied evader in occupied France wearing civilian clothes.

As it was, the first cargo of evaders to the forest wasn't discovered and the vehicle pulled up at Hallouin's lodge. The doors to the van were opened and the evaders emerged. Peloquin recalls that 'Mr Lucien Boussa and Jean de Blommaert were together at the start.' They both greeted the evaders briefly and warmly before leading them into the forest and out of sight of any passing German.

Within Fréteval Forest, an area had been chosen – roughly eight hundred metres from the lodge of Hallouin, who was harbouring Boussa – where the initial camp would be located. It was near the farm of Bellande and appeared the ideal location for the first thirty evaders. It was in a relatively thickly wooded area, hidden by trees and foliage, and just 100 metres from a natural spring, though they could never rule out the threat of a nosy German patrol. However there was a slight slope leading up to the border of the forest which would enable those hiding an easy surveillance of the immediate approaches to the camp and a decent vantage point to scan for unwanted visitors.

As they made their way through the scrub, for all but a few of the initial thirty evaders it was their first view of the primitive camp that was to be their home for the next few months. Although it was June, it was a breezy 12° C, hardly the most welcoming environment as they viewed their rudimentary tents constructed beneath the foliage, alongside the basic tables and chairs made out of tree trunks and branches. Boussa had managed to procure from local farmers some milk, butter, eggs, meat, flour and vegetables for the evaders, and this provided the basis of their rations.

Despite the crude living prospects, Peloquin immediately appreciated the environment: 'The forest was very beautiful … They had nice wide paths and the trees were pruned back and taken care of. I couldn't believe that it could be done but it sure was. The French were very proud of their forests and took very good care of them.'

Before leaving the thirty airmen – the first evaders in the camp – Boussa and de Blommaert read them the riot act. No weapons were permitted within the camp (if any of the evaders had been caught with weapons by the Germans they would have certainly been shot as members of the Resistance). Fires could be lit but only charcoal (provided by a local farmer) could be used as it gave off little smoke. Any alcohol within the camp had to be entrusted to one man, who'd keep guard of it. Sentries should be posted at all times at the entrances to the forest, especially at dawn, and would warn of strangers by giving a whistle (a few short bars of 'This is The Army, Mr Jones' announced that new camp members were approaching). Also, each man was given an 'escape kit', consisting of rations and a small amount of local currency in case the camp was compromised.

Apart from the small group of Resistance helpers, only Dr Feyssier from Cloyes and a hairdresser, Albert Barillet, would be allowed to enter the forest. All communication, especially at night, had to be conducted by whispering as a raised voice could mean the difference between life or death. 'We had to be very careful. We didn't dare talk at night,' said Ray Worrall. 'It was summertime, and voices carry at night. It was generally understood we had to talk in whispers at night.'

And no one was to try and escape and make it back to England alone: fear of capture and subsequent interrogation that would betray the camp was too great a risk. Not only that, they would surely face summary execution at the hands of the Germans as, in October 1942, Hitler had passed the notorious Commando Order that decreed any non-uniformed soldier taken prisoner would be treated as a spy, tortured and executed.

If the Germans didn't shoot them, the Resistance would. 'If anyone tried to escape they would have been shot by the Resistance,' remembered Ray Worrall. 'The Resistance said, "If you try to escape on your own, if the Germans don't get you, we will."'

With the evaders left in no doubt about the rules, Boussa and de Blommaert left them and crept away.

Tomorrow there would be more evaders to take into the forest.

CHAPTER 14

ENEMY ON THE EDGE

The final trek to Fréteval Forest was, in many ways, the most dangerous part of the evaders' journey. It had to be conducted on open roads or across fields in a part of occupied France where German units were stationed and where patrols frequently roamed around Cloyes. The arrival of the first few groups saw them get off the train at Châteaudun (or rendezvous at the station if they had walked there like Beauchesne and Vickerman) and then, from a relay set up in a little grocery store owned by the Coeuret family, they would be taken to Fréteval along indirect country roads.

Every effort was made to deceive enemy surveillance and protect the evaders, escorts and guides, who constantly changed routes and the mode of travel to avoid detection. Most frequently the evaders would travel by foot from

Châteaudun to Fréteval but sometimes bicycles or cars would be used and, in some instances, even horse-drawn carriages. If the evaders were led across fields they were given pitchforks and hoes to give the impression they were farm workers.

Neave wrote that, 'Over all of us hung the fear that if the Germans knew that they were losing the war, they would turn to brutal methods and spare no one, even in uniform. It was foreseen that retreating Germans might have ragged nerves; Oradour-sur-Glane provided tragic evidence that this foresight was correct.'[99]

Oradour-sur-Glane was a small market town, roughly twenty miles from the city of Limoges. In June 1944, it had largely remained peaceful during the German occupation of France and, as such, it had become a safe haven for refugees such as Jews and exiles from the Lorraine region. The only real change the town had seen since the outbreak of war was the absence of men, most of whom had been sent to work in Germany. Life appeared to be going on as normal and the war seemed a distant distraction. As one resident explained, 'Really, we sort of thought that we were – that we weren't part of the war. We thought that we wouldn't be concerned by the war.'[100]

Saturday 10 June 1944 promised to be just like any other Saturday. It was market day in the town and would be busy because tobacco rations were being given out and children also arrived from outlying hamlets for their vaccinations.

Nearby German troops were moving north through occupied France to counter the advance made by the Allies

Left: Airey Neave: MI9's architect for the most audacious escape and evasion plan of World War II.   © *Getty Images*

Right: Baron Jean de Blommaert: One of the most daring figures of the Belgian Resistance and a highly valued agent of MI9. Parachuted into France in 1944, he was instrumental in setting up the camp at Fréteval.

© *The Brayley Estate/Lorraine Vickerman*

Above: During World War II factories were building 28 Wellington bombers a week. In contrast it took two years to train the crew to fly them. Any downed aircrew brought back to Britain would therefore save on time and money.

© Getty Images

Right: The iconic Lancaster bomber under construction. It flew over 156,000 sorties in World War II but at a terrible cost: of every 100 airmen who joined Bomber Command only 41 escaped unscathed.

© Getty Images

Above: Lancaster bombers dropped more than 600,000 tons of bombs on the enemy during World War II. Targets included communication and transport networks in the run-up to D-Day, but this also hindered escape lines for Allied airmen across Europe.

Below: As aircraft departed, crews would take one last look at Britain below them. 'You think you'd never see the UK again. We were off to, maybe, get killed,' recalled flight engineer Ray Worrall.

Top: Accommodation was basic, often no more than tarpaulins scavenged from local farms by the Resistance and draped over branches or timber.

Below left: Evaders did what they could to ensure personal hygiene. A spring provided bathing water and a barber from the local town visited once a week, but the evaders had to wear the same clothes for up to three months. Delousing powder was dropped in by parachute.

Below right: Each airman had an 'escape kit' issued to them for a mission over Europe. In the forest camp the needle and thread was a useful tool in sewing together material for more makeshift tents as the numbers of camp inmates increased.

Above: Nobody remembered the food on offer in the camp with affection. Cooked over a charcoal fire to avoid smoke being seen, the menu consisted of whatever the Resistance could smuggle into the forest.

Left: By the middle of August 1944, over 150 men were being fed from local supplies supplemented by food dropped by parachute. Cigarettes were also parachuted in but never the one thing the English evaders really wanted: tea.

Above: Boredom was alleviated by card schools and the Americans even created a rudimentary golf-course within the forest with clubs and balls fashioned out of wood.

Below: Radio contact with MI9 allowed the evaders to prepare for parachute drops as well as keeping them informed about the Allied advance following D-Day and the potential date of their liberation.

Above: All the evaders arrived in the forest camp wearing civilian clothing provided by the Resistance. It meant that if they were discovered by the Germans they would be shot as spies as they no longer had uniform protection. © *The Brayley Estate/Lorraine Vickerman*

Below: French Resistance fighters at a farmhouse near Chateaudun in August 1944. Their bravery, discretion and loyalty helped keep the evaders in Fréteval fed, watered and protected. © *Getty Images*

The last survivor of the Operation Sherwood, British RAF veteran Raymond Worrall, now in his mid-nineties, revisits the site of the secret camp in the Fréteval forest. In the second image, he is accompanied by Belgian Air Component pilots who were recreating the camp ahead of commemorations.

after the D-Day landings, amongst them the elite *Das Reich* division. Recently arrived from the Eastern Front, and bringing with them Eastern Front methods (on 9 June they'd hanged ninety-nine Resistance fighters in nearby Tulle and only stopped at that number when they ran out of rope and a priest begged them to spare the lives of others), their orders were to seek out and destroy Resistance forces who, buoyed by news filtering through about the Allied invasion, were becoming increasingly audacious and effective.

On 10 June at approximately 2 pm, in what is generally agreed by historians as a premeditated action, about two hundred German soldiers of the *Das Reich* division, under the command of *Sturmbannführer* Adolf Diekmann, encircled Oradour-sur-Glane. All roads were sealed off and all the inhabitants were ordered to assemble in the Champ de Foire, a square in the centre of the town, for an identity check. As this was happening, other German soldiers in armoured cars rounded up men working in nearby farms and fields. Few in the town felt any reason not to co-operate – after all, this appeared to be a routine identity check. But when SS soldiers began searching shops and homes and dragging people found in them to the square, the mood changed.

Other soldiers burst in to a school for refugee children and ordered them all to join the adults. They all co-operated, except for eight-year-old Roger Godfrin, who ran through the back door of the school building and hid in a field of grass.

While Godfrin hid, the townsfolk in the square were

separated with all the men being shepherded in to six barns and the women and children to the church. One of the men taken to a barn was Jean-Marcel Darthout. 'We were laughing,' he said. 'We weren't afraid. We were thinking of the next day's soccer match.'[101] Once in the barns, the men started talking amongst themselves, oblivious to an SS soldier mounting a machine gun on a tripod outside. Moments later came the command to fire and a hail of bullets cut through the barns and the men. Then soldiers entered the barns to shoot those still alive and cover the bodies with straw, before setting fire to the buildings. Remarkably, six men survived by hiding under dead bodies. One of the survivors was Darthout. 'We felt the bullets, which brought me down. Everyone was on top of me. And they were still firing. And there was shouting. And crying. I had a friend who was lying on top of me and who was moaning. And then it was over. No more shots. And they came at us, stepping on us. And with a rifle they finished us off. They finished off the buddy who was on top of me. I felt it when he died.'[102] As the building burned, the six men escaped into another barn and then towards the edge of town and safety. Not all made it. Pierre-Henri Poutaraud was shot as he fled.

Meanwhile, the women and children were imprisoned in the church. They were now beside themselves with fear having heard the gunfire and flames licking through nearby buildings. At 5 pm, two German soldiers entered the church carrying a large chest, which they placed on the altar and retreated, trailing behind them a long fuse.

At the door to the church, the soldiers lit the fuse then left the church, locking the door shut behind them. Moments later the chest exploded, blowing out the church windows, filling it with smoke and instantly killing many of those inside. Anybody not killed by the explosion was shot by German soldiers, who stormed back into the church and sprayed it with machine-gun fire.

Then they piled wooden pews on the bodies, poured petrol over them and set the church alight. Only one person escaped death in the church, forty-seven-year-old Madame Margueritte Rouffanche. She had been ordered from her home along with her husband, son, two daughters and granddaughter and waited in the square until they were separated. This is her testimony to a military tribunal in Bordeaux in 1953.

The first group that I was in was taken under armed guard to the church. It consisted of all the women from the village, especially mothers, who entered the House of God carrying their babies in their arms or pushing them in their prams. All the schoolchildren were there as well. We must have numbered several hundred.

Shoved together in the holy place, we became more and more worried as we awaited the end of the preparations being made for us. At about 4 pm some soldiers, about twenty years old, placed a sort of bulky box in the nave, near the choir, from which strings were lit and the flames passed to the apparatus which suddenly produced a strong explosion with dense, black, suffocating smoke billowing out. The women and children, half-choked and screaming with fright rushed towards the parts of the church where the air was still breathable. The door of the sacristy was then broken in by the violent thrust of one horrified group. I followed in after but gave up and sat on a stair. My daughter came and sat down with me. When the Germans noticed that this room had been broken into they savagely shot down those who had tried to find shelter there. My daughter was killed near me by a bullet fired from outside. I owe my life to the idea I had to shut my eyes and pretend to be dead. Firing burst out in the church then straw, faggots and chairs were thrown pell-mell onto bodies lying on the stone slabs.

I had escaped from the killing and was without injury, so I made use of a smoke cloud to slip behind the altar. In this part of the church there are three windows. I made for the widest one in the middle and, with the help of a stool used to light the candles, I tried to reach it. I don't know how but my strength was multiplied. I heaved myself up to it as best I could and threw myself out of the opening that was offered to me through the already shattered window. I jumped about nine feet down. When I looked up I saw I had been followed in my climb by a woman holding out her baby to me. She fell down next to me but the Germans, alerted by the cries of the baby, machine-gunned us. The woman and the mite were killed and I too was injured as I made it to a neighbouring garden and hid among some rows of peas and waited anxiously for someone to come to help me. That wasn't until the following day at 5 pm.

A total of 642 people were massacred at Oradour-sur-Glane, amongst them over four hundred women and children. Only six people escaped.* The most common explanation for the massacre, following evidence presented at the International Military Tribunals at Nuremberg in 1946 and Bordeaux in 1953, as well as subsequent West German investigations of the officers of *Das Reich*, suggests that the commander, SS-Major General Heinz Bernard Lammerding and the commander of the 1st Battalion, SS-Major Adolf Diekmann, received intelligence that the villagers were assisting the Resistance.

Another theory is that French collaborators misled the Germans, perhaps deliberately, into believing that French insurgents were holding the kidnapped German officer, SS-Major Helmut Kämpfe, in the town and had planned to kill him (or, indeed, had already killed him), and this was a reprisal. To this day, as the ruins of the town stand in memorial to those killed that day, the real reason why the

---

* In 1981, authorities in the German Democratic Republic arrested and prosecuted Heinz Barth, a former SS sergeant and platoon commander whose soldiers were among those who shot the men of Oradour-sur-Glane. An East Berlin court sentenced Barth to life in prison. Released in 1997, Barth died in 2007 at the age of eighty-six. In January 2014, an eighty-eight-year old man from Cologne, identified as Werner C – his last name withheld in accordance with German privacy laws – was charged by prosecutors in Dortmund with the murder of twenty-five people, committed with a group, and with aiding and abetting the murder of several hundred people during the Oradour-sur-Glane massacre. However, in December 2014 the case was thrown out with the court citing a lack of evidence. Prosecutors eventually identified twelve members of the regiment who were still alive after trawling through files of the Stasi secret police in the former communist east that came to light after German reunification in 1990. Probes were opened against seven of them but prosecutor Andreas Brendel, head of the central Nazi war crimes investigation unit in the western city of Dortmund, stated that none of the other suspects had been charged. The other five soldiers have already served sentences in France.

massacre at Oradour-sur-Glane occurred remains disputed and will probably always remain so.

Neave was right to fear such reprisals against any of his evaders, or indeed the communities of families hiding them. The tide of war had been turning against the Germans for some time by June 1944 and whilst it was unlikely the regular German soldier would resort to such brutality, the potential actions of the Gestapo and secret police couldn't be so easily predicted.

As it happened, on 12 June, less than a week after the first evaders made their way into the forest and a week before Vickerman began his journey to Fréteval, the camp had its first – and most serious – threat to security.

More new arrivals had been hidden within the forest, among them Bill Brayley who was busily helping the evaders already in the forest make the camp more hospitable. On 11 June, he was joined by fellow Canadian flying officers W.F. Bender and R.B. Gordon. They had travelled from Paris with their guides, who included Virginia d'Albert Lake, her husband Philippe and Germaine Méllison (known as 'Annie').

The whole group had convened in Dourdan, about fifty miles from Châteaudun, and then walked fifteen miles to Denonville, east of Chartres, where they spent the night hiding in a barn. The following day the party decided to split up to avoid detection and Annie took Bender and Gordon straight to the forest camp without incident. Meanwhile, the Lakes and their 'packages' prepared to travel to Fréteval the next day. These men would also be split into groups to avoid any unwanted attention: Virginia would take the two Canadians and four Americans while Philippe would be responsible for two South Africans.

On the morning of 12 June, a local Resistance member, Jean Méret, came to meet Virginia. He arrived in a horse-drawn cart, his mode of transport for the evaders, hidden beneath sacks and straw. Sitting beside him on the cart would be another Resistance member, Robert Poupard, and between them Michelle, a Parisian Underground worker. Ahead of the cart cycled Resistance member Daniel Cogneu from Châteaudun and Alfred Hickman of the USAAF, himself an evader. In her bag Virginia was not only carrying food tickets and 127,000 French francs, but also a pencil sketch of their route and a map of the Fréteval camp. It was the most incriminating evidence that she was working with the Resistance and proof she was an enemy of Germany, and it would also would give away to the Germans the secret of Fréteval camp if it fell into enemy hands. Virginia knew the risks but also knew how to look after herself. Or so she thought.

Born Virginia Roush on 4 June 1910 in Dayton, Ohio, she had spent the years immediately prior to the war teaching at her mother's private country day school in St Petersburg, Florida. In 1936, she travelled to England to attend an educational convention and, while there, took the opportunity to travel to France for a short break. In France she met a dashing young man from Brittany, Philippe d'Albert Lake, and fell in love. Returning to Florida, Virginia told her mother of her plans to marry the

Frenchman. 'My mother was devastated,' she recalled. 'She stayed in bed for a week. She didn't want me to marry a Frenchman and move away.'[103]

On 1 May 1937, Virginia and Philippe married in Florida and honeymooned in New York City before setting sail for Europe where they settled in Philippe's apartment at 57 Rue de Bellechasse in Paris. On the outbreak of war Virginia began a diary. Her first entry describes how she had adjusted 'to this new strange state of living, diving in a kind of suspension, just waiting and hoping, while time itself seems to have neither a yesterday nor a tomorrow'.[104]

With Philippe now mobilized in the army, they spent less and less time together. They bought a small country weekend cottage in the tiny village of Nesles-la-Vallée, and watched in horror as Germany invaded France and an armistice was signed between the two countries. 'Thus, we have begun a new existence under the Nazi regime! We are beginning to experience those regulations that have shocked us for the last few years knowing of their existence in Germany! What a blow for France and for the whole civilised world,' Virginia wrote in her diary on 23 June 1940.

The next three years were spent in occupied France with Philippe often spending great lengths of time away with the army, leaving Virginia constantly fretting about his welfare. Any periods of leave saw the two of them either cycling through France or spending time together at their isolated cottage retreat. It was here, in the autumn of 1943, that they were approached by the local baker who wanted to speak privately with Philippe and promptly drove him to his bakery. Later that day the phone rang in their cottage and Virginia answered to find Philippe on the end of the line asking her to come to the bakery immediately. She could hear the excitement in his voice.

She went to the shop and was led into the store-room where three young men sat beside Philippe. Virginia quickly realised they were downed American airmen and, with her husband, she now had a compelling but potentially dangerous decision to make. They debated into the night. 'We talked over the whole evening, discussed the boys and made a big decision: we would work in the Underground. Dangerous, yes, but we would be careful. It would be worth every risk run just to meet more boys like those tonight and lead them from right under the German noses back home and the work yet to be accomplished,' she wrote after the war.[105]

Joe Peloquin, one of those in Fréteval and someone who was looked after by Virginia while evading capture, recalled meeting her while hiding out in France. 'I did get to talk to her a little. She told me that she was an American, too, from Florida, and had married a Frenchman prior to the war and felt very strongly about helping her own countrymen as well.'

Within days, Philippe and Virginia were working as part of the Comet Line from their main home back in Paris. Virginia would convey downed airmen from the Gare du Nord to secret hideouts in the city, and she would quiz airmen on their way through the Comet Line to ensure they weren't German agents posing as Allied pilots. Virginia had a list of questions she posed to the downed airmen ranging from Who is 'Babe' Ruth? (answer: a baseball player) and What is a grouper? (a group captain) to What are two bits? (25 cents). Each question was specific to American, Canadian or British culture and carefully angled to uncover a spy. If she found one she turned him over to the Resistance. The results were not always pretty.

Becoming increasingly bold and confident, Virginia hid airmen in her apartment and would even take them for guided walks around Paris, convinced they would go stir crazy holed up there whilst they waited for the next leg of their journey. One of the downed airmen who spent time in Virginia and Philippe's Paris apartment was Yankus, who reflected on his first meeting with Virginia after being shot down over France and shepherded to Paris before being transported to Fréteval. 'There we were, walking into this apartment after some pretty hairy experiences and being greeted by this beautiful woman who said, "Hi, fellas, how're you doing?" She had no fear whatsoever.'[106]

Yankus described how Virginia would look after downed airmen in Paris, often in full view of the Germans. 'She took us out for a walk in the streets. She put her arms in ours like we were old friends and told us not to speak, to pretend we were French and deaf and dumb. She told us to take our hands out of our pockets, because that was a giveaway that we were Americans. And she taught us how to eat like Frenchmen – you know, to eat with both hands, knife in one, fork in the other. One day we were at a restaurant and she said, "See the Gestapo over there? They are watching you eat.'"[107] Another airman looked after by Philippe and Virginia was Englishman Pete Berry, told by Philippe that he 'should get plenty of excitement soon', when Berry expressed a desire to join the Resistance.

When D-Day happened, having spent months working on the Comet Line, Virginia and Philippe had a number of Allied airmen at their apartment and knew they would have to act quickly to ensure their safety. After the war he said:

It had been agreed that on D-Day we were to join the camp ourselves, so we decided to attempt the trip on foot. Virginia and I left Paris on 7 June with three convoy girls and eleven men. The girls were Anne-Marie, Michelle and Annie. Virginia, myself and one of the boys started out on bicycles, the others took a suburban train that still ran to Dourdan, 25 miles from Paris. We all met at Dourdan and started to walk towards Châteaudun in small groups of two or three. It was not an easy job and even the weather was against us. The second day, owing to our procession of sixteen people being spotted ... we decided to split up into small groups which would individually reach a rendezvous point short of Châteaudun where we hoped that Jean [Méret] could have us picked up by some vehicle. Virginia, one boy and myself took the bicycles and went ahead in order to establish contact with the camp. We established contact with the first intermediary at Châteaudun. He said he could arrange for a cart to go to our rendezvous point the next morning and could also have me and the boy accompanied to the camp the first thing in the morning. It was agreed that Virginia would go with the cart in order to identify the men at the meeting point. The next day the cart met seven men and Michele at the rendezvous. Annie and the others had gone direct to a certain farm that she knew, and Anne-Marie and one man had walked straight to Châteaudun. Six of the men and Michele got in the cart. Virginia and one man cycled a short distance ahead.[108]

Leaving that morning for the camp at Fréteval, Virginia had been buoyed by the sight of formation after formation of American B-17 Flying Fortress bombers flying overhead signalling the ever-increasing dominance in the air of the Allies. With the aid of rudimentary maps, they made their way down winding country roads towards the camp. 'The route was so complicated, so many turnings and cross-roads, that we had to study the map carefully in order not to lose our way,' she wrote in her memoirs. As the end of the hazardous and dangerous journey was in sight she began to breathe easier. Cycling beside her, the American Alfred Hickman turned to her and said, 'Isn't it wonderful that we're nearly there.' They rounded a bend with the cart following about 50 yards behind.

A few minutes later, in the distance, a large black car turned abruptly off a main road ahead and began heading in their direction along the narrow country road. 'I suddenly felt nervous. What would such a car be doing on such a desolate road?' Virginia thought. By this point, the cart had rounded the bend and Jean could also spot the car ahead of them.

She pulled to the side of the road to let the car pass but it slowed to a stop. There were three German policemen inside. As they got out one of them ordered Virginia off her bike and asked for identity papers. Handing them over, he couldn't fail to notice that her papers stated that she was born an American citizen. 'I had never pretended otherwise', she later wrote, 'as it would have been impossible considering the strong accent with which I spoke French.'

"'What are you doing in the region when your identity card states that you live in Paris?" he asked gruffly, in perfect French.

"'We have been searching the farms for fruit and eggs," I lied.

"'Ah," his voice rose with interest, "you have an English accent. I see now your card states that you were born in the United States."

"'Yes, but I am French by marriage." I lied. "I took my husband's nationality when I married. I have the right to circulate."

"'Perhaps." Then, he quickly added, glancing back to Al [Hickman] and the stranger*, "Are you with these two men?"

"'No, we're riding together quite by accident; they joined me from a side road further back." This was my only chance of escape, but all the time I was conscious of

---

* They had been joined on this final leg of the journey by another cyclist whom nobody knew.

Al's coat that was very much in evidence in my basket, and it was a coat which very obviously matched the trousers he was wearing. I wondered if they had noticed it.

'I tried to appear unconcerned and prepared to mount my bicycle, but I was tense and trembling. I knew that this moment was a climax in my life. These few seconds would prove the success or failure of my effort to escape. I hopefully pushed down on the pedal.

'"Stop," he roared out. "Not so fast."

'Something broke inside me. I knew somehow that it was all over. There was no more reason to hope. The sun that only a few minutes ago was so bright and warm, now seem eclipsed by a grey fog. Disappointment and fear clothed me in a hot vapour. Sweat started in my armpits; my scalp tingled. I had no choice but to stand there in the centre of the dusty road, grip my handle bars and wait.'

Behind them, about thirty yards back, the cart had stopped, realising what was happening up ahead. Casting a discreet glance back at it, Virginia saw that the airmen who were hidden beneath the sacks and the straw had started to stealthily climb out and make their way off the road and hide in the undergrowth. For Hickman, however, there was no hiding place, especially when one of the Germans noticed the coat in Virginia's basket and realised it matched his trousers. But before he questioned Hickman he grabbed Virginia's handbag and began rifling through its contents. 'I suddenly recalled something which made terror clutch at my heart,' she wrote, knowing she had broken one of the Resistance's cardinal rules. 'Before leaving Paris I had disposed of every bit of incriminating evidence, but I still had the list of addresses of the Underground at Châteaudun that Philippe had given me only yesterday, prior to my leaving alone to make the necessary contacts. The feeling of guilt that overcame me was worse than anything I had yet suffered.'

This list noted all the people she had met the day before, names that could identify virtually all Resistance in the area and their families. Virginia was all too aware of what the Germans might do to them. Furthermore, there was a map leading directly to Fréteval camp. At that precise moment, the fate of all those men and the entire Sherwood plan was at risk. One of those in the camp later recalled hearing she had been captured: 'We all knew that if Virginia talked, the Germans would show up and we probably would be killed.'[109]

Virginia could only watch as the German picked through her handbag. He saw the map, food tickets, the envelope containing money and then the piece of paper on which were written all the names of local Resistance operatives. 'He hesitated over this, then, to my amazement, he put everything back into my bag, addresses and all, and handed it back to me!'

It was an astonishing stroke of good fortune as the German switched his attention from Virginia's handbag to Hickman. As he moved towards Hickman, Virginia hid the handbag under her jacket and slowly opened it. She located a piece of paper, hoping it was the list of Resistance members, and began quietly tearing it into tiny pieces.

The German police officer found nothing of interest

on Hickman with the exception of his dog tag which proved he was a serviceman and not a spy, and ordered them both to get into the car that took them directly to the Feldgendarmerie at Châteaudun. Here they were taken into a busy room where the policeman who had arrested them began discussing the case with his superiors. At this moment, Virginia realised nobody was actually watching her. She fished out all of the torn pieces of paper from her handbag, put them in her mouth and, after struggling to chew them, eventually swallowed them, to her great relief.

Moments later, the German returned to question her and grabbed her handbag, emptying the contents onto the desk. It was obvious he was looking for the list of addresses. Not able to find them, he turned on Virginia demanding to know where the paper with the list of addresses was. Virginia denied all knowledge of it, but he saw one tiny scrap of paper that had fallen on the floor. He immediately accused Virginia of eating the list. She didn't deny it. Later, while under guard, one of the policemen told her, 'You'd better tell everything you know and don't do any lying. That's the only thing that might save you. As it is, you will probably be shot tomorrow morning. We haven't had time to judge people since the invasion.' Virginia resolved to not say anything.

Shortly afterwards she was joined by Hickman, who had returned from his own interrogation, and they were both taken by car to Chartres where Virginia was thrown into a cold, damp prison with just a smelly straw mattress to sleep on and a bucket for a toilet. She had no idea what was going to happen to her. She had hoped, vainly, that during her drive to the prison her husband and the Resistance might launch an ambush and spring her from her captors.

Two days later she was taken to the Gestapo headquarters in Chartres but didn't divulge any information during her questioning, causing her interrogator to burst out in frustration: 'To think that you dare save the men who cause so much death and destruction. You have been helping murderers!' A few days later she was transferred back to Paris and sent to the Prison de Fresnes. Here she was imprisoned for seven weeks in a flea-ridden cell.

Questioned just twice by the Germans during her time there she managed to keep her secrets safe, despite often seeing other prisoners being dragged through the prison corridors suffering the effects of torture.

After seven weeks she was taken to the notorious Romainville Prison on the outskirts of Paris. It was a holding place for prisoners before they were deported to Germany. On 15 August 1944, just 10 days before the Allied liberation of Paris, Virginia was transported to Ravensbrück concentration camp, 50 miles north of Berlin. (On the train journey, during a brief stop, she met a fellow Resistance operative who told her that Philippe had managed to escape to England.) Ravensbrück was predominantly for women and children, and Heinrich Himmler, the head of the SS, had a particular interest in the camp. Here inmates suffered the full Nazi culture of brutality: a fenced-in, heavily guarded pit of starvation with forced abortions, murder of new-borns, grisly medical experiments, sterilizations, routine shootings, lethal injections and gassings. Stepping off the train Virginia saw the inmates for the first time: 'horrible-looking creatures, thin and haggard, with huge, open, festering sores on their stocking-less legs ... It was sinister, unreal, unbelievable.'

Virginia spent the rest of the war in Ravensbrück where she was given the prison number 57631. Working nearly twelve hours a day in dysentery- and typhus-ridden surroundings and fearing the onset of a bitter winter, her only aim was survival. All around she witnessed depravity and death, but she was determined to survive. By eating the list of addresses of Resistance workers, she had saved the lives of many men, women and children, as well as the Allied airmen at Fréteval. Now, she was determined to save her own life.

After seven months in Ravensbrück – seven months of starvation, toil, freezing cold, the constant threat of brutality by guards, the fear that every day might be your last – Virginia was sent to an internment camp at Libenau near the Swiss border. Two months later, on 21 April 1945, she was liberated by Free French Forces. She weighed just 75 pounds but had not divulged any information and had kept the secrets of the French Resistance and the camp at Fréteval Forest intact.* When asked in an interview how she survived in the concentration camps, Virginia said, 'It was a question of will. You could never give in. The women who cried at night were usually dead in the morning.'[110]

Virginia's arrest was the first time the camp was almost

---

* After the war she opened an antiques business with Philippe in Cancaval, Brittany. Honoured by a number of governments for her efforts during the war, including the French Legion d'Honneur in 1989, she died peacefully on 20 September 1997. Philippe passed away on 10 February 2000.

compromised. It wasn't to be the last and it showed the potential vulnerability of the hideout. Consequently, in the immediate aftermath of her arrest, extra sentries were posted around the camp. Boussa, distraught at the news of Virginia's arrest, and not knowing she had swallowed the list of Resistance addresses, feared they might be discovered at any moment and put everyone on high alert, fearing German attacks and reprisals. 'They could come at any time,' he said, and got Hallouin to provide an early warning system should German troops advance en masse. If he lit a fire in the grounds of his cottage everyone knew they had to flee.

At the time of Virginia's arrest, the camp consisted of less than fifty evaders and fifteen roughly constructed tents made from tarpaulins. Within days, however, the camp began to grow considerably as more evaders were moved there from Paris or brought from the nearby countryside. 'Every day the Underground would bring in new people, sometimes as many as ten at a time,' Peloquin said. 'Jean [de Blommaert] would bring some and then Lucien [Boussa] would leave for a few days and then come back with more.'

But as the number of camp inmates grew, so did the problems of looking after them.

CHAPTER 15

THE CAMP

By the middle of June 1944, about fifty British and American airmen were camping in the foliage and undergrowth of the forest. It was a basic and primitive way of life. Cliff Hallett entered the camp in June and his first impressions of what greeted him indicate the nature of the camp: 'We walked in and it was an amazing sight. There were tables and chairs all roughly hewn out of tree trunks and branches, pots and pans and cooking fires and makeshift tents. I couldn't stop thinking of the teddy bear's picnic and the boy scouts.'[111]

Ian Murray was one of Ray Worrall's crew and he recalled his first sight of the camp:

I was taken by bicycle to the edge of a wood, where we hid our machines and waited. Presently a voice called

'Come this way', so I left my friends and followed into the thick wood. The woods were so thick that I could not see more than 5 yards through the foliage and we had to stoop as we walked along the narrow path. The entrance was invisible from the road outside the woods, and even after I had been there a few days I still had difficulty in finding it. There was dead silence as we walked, but soon we came to a small clearing in the centre of the woods. Several tents were erected and about fifty men were sitting and lounging around, talking quietly or playing cards. One or two were whittling sticks with pocket knives. Most of them were dressed in tattered civilian clothes, but a few wore RAF battle dress and flying boots. Suddenly one in battle dress gave a cry and sprang up. It was my skipper. At once three others rushed over and we were all hugging each other and laughing until someone warned us that we were making too much noise.

News of the Normandy invasion had spread amongst them, the latest information brought into the camp by the newest arrivals. It created an air of excitement but it also made everyone tense, as they were all aware of the Germans nearby and the unpredictable nature of their retreat. There was every possibility that even if the German soldiers stationed close by in Cloyes didn't come into the forest to search for them then perhaps they would retreat into it as the Allies advanced across France. The prospect of being discovered by retreating and defeated Germans with little to lose was not an attractive proposition. Neither was the potential of being caught up in a terrifying firefight between the Germans and the Allies.

From the moment he had arrived in the camp on 7 June, having been made camp commander by de Blommaert, Berry ('A rather cocky little chap,' according to Worrall) realised discipline, order and routine was vital if the men were to co-exist successfully and, more importantly, secretly for however long they needed to be there. 'There were certain camp laws,' according to Berry, 'which if necessary were enforced by stoppages of cigarettes or camp fatigues. Otherwise the camp was run on democratic lines and except for myself, all rank and seniority was washed out. All had the same food, duties and fatigues, and were controlled by the same laws. Every man was informed on entering camp what this law was, and his rights and privileges.'

One of the main rules of the camp was that there should be no weapons (although Berry himself had a revolver, which he kept concealed). It was crucial that, if discovered, the Allied evaders shouldn't be armed. If they were, they could be classified as spies and face death. Another reason not to be armed, according to Boussa, was that if the camp was overrun by Germans he feared the Allies might take 'the easy route out' and commit suicide rather than face the Germans. As it happened, the only weapon apparent to everyone in the camp was an enormous cudgel. This wasn't to be used to repel any German troops breaching the forest, instead it was given to one of the 'reception committee' when greeting new arrivals.

When Boussa met the newcomers, he did so half a mile away from the camp to protect its security. He'd also screen them to check they were not German infiltrators. Boussa would refer to himself as Lucien Belgrade during these first encounters. Everyone in MI9 and the Resistance knew that the Germans in Berlin had ordered spies to slip into the Allied escape organisations. As he interrogated the men, Boussa would always say, 'If you are not what you seem to be, you won't live long.' Once he had vetted them they were permitted to enter the forest where they would be met by Berry and a group of other evaders, one of them with the cudgel. More vetting would take place and anybody not answering the tough questions correctly would face being dispatched quietly, quickly and efficiently by the man with the cudgel. Such was the work of the Resistance outside the forest, however, and the due diligence they carried out on any prospective forest inmate, that the cudgel was never used.

Despite the insistence that the evaders should not have any weapons, it was decided by de Blommaert that a small group of them should launch a raiding party on one of the German ammunition dumps located close to the forest to secure ammunition for the Resistance. It was 12 June and Brayley had just arrived in the forest camp. One of the first to befriend him was Peloquin who, despite coming from Maine, was of French–Canadian descent and, together, the two of them were chosen to accompany Berry, de Blommaert and Jubault out of the forest, under cover of darkness, to steal some ammunition. It was a risky operation:

the Germans now routinely policed the perimeter of the forest, passing every 15 minutes or so, and the ammunition dump was located 400 yards away on the curve of a road, which they also patrolled. Carefully making their way through the scrub to the edge of the woods, the five men lay down. Enough light was being cast by the June half-moon for them to see the ammunition dump in the distance and carry out their task, but it was also enough to enable any passing German patrol to spot them.

They scouted the road and waited for the next patrol to pass. As it approached they ducked down silently beneath the bracken and waited for a couple of minutes. Certain it was out of sight, they ran across the road, into the next field, and sprinted to the ammunition. It wasn't guarded: the Germans felt that the routine patrols were enough of a deterrent to the local Resistance. They hadn't counted on five men springing from the nearby forest.

They quickly filled their bags with 48 grenades and as much .303 ammunition as they could carry. They soon realised that it wasn't German ammunition they were stealing but British Army property, the spoils of Dunkirk. In that respect, thought Peloquin, they were taking what was rightfully theirs. Everything went to plan until a German patrol vehicle broke the silence. They didn't have time to make it back to the forest, especially now that they were weighed down with ammunition. There was no option but to lie flat on the ground behind whatever cover they could find and hope. All five hit the deck instantly. The sound of the vehicle got closer. The five held their breath, desperate to look up to see what was happening. They heard the vehicle pull to a stop and German voices drifting across the night. A door opened, and they heard footsteps across the asphalt. The footsteps stopped, a zip was undone, followed by the unmistakable sound of a man pissing. The five evaders looked at each other, desperate not to make a sound. They held their positions until they heard the zip being done up, the footsteps marching back to the vehicle, the door being closed shut and the car accelerate away. Finally, the men could breathe. Gathering their bounty, they got to their feet and scurried back the way they came, diving into the cover of the forest and making their way back to the camp. The following day the grenades and ammunition were hidden at various sites in the forest, ready for the Resistance when they needed it.

One of those in the raiding party, Brayley, had been reported missing since 10 April 1944 after his Halifax bomber had been shot down. He had already spent two months being hidden and ferried about from location to location by the Resistance before he arrived at Fréteval. Helping with the construction and maintenance of the camp, he began writing a diary of daily life in the forest. On 15 June he wrote: 'It is decided to adopt the name *Escadrille Soixante-neuf* [Sixty-nine) with the flying helmet insignia and the 100-franc membership card.' The name was well chosen, and it had a deliberate sexual connotation; by now sixty-nine men were in the camp, sharing twenty-five tents. Sleeping arrangements were cosy to say the least. Two days later, on 17 June, Brayley wrote: 'Arrival of two barrels of wine, one white, one rosay [sic]. We had a ball.'

While the arrival of alcohol was welcome, deliveries of food were more important and right from the start getting hold of food for the airmen was difficult for the Resistance. It could easily give the game away. 'As the camp grew in size, provisions become de Blommaert's most serious headache,' Neave wrote, overseeing operations in London.[112] Brayley, in his diary entries for 17–21 June, confirms just how serious the problem was becoming: 'More and more wounded, tired airmen pour into the camp. Bags and blankets are at a premium. The food and cigarette situation begins to get worse.'

De Blommaert compiled a list of the daily food requirements needed to sustain the men in the camp. '500 grammes of bread per man per day. 1 kilo of butter for 12 men each day. 1 litre of milk per man per day. 2 eggs per man per day. 400 grammes of potatoes per man per day. 100 grammes of meat per man per day. 8 cigarettes per man per day. If possible, fresh fruit and vegetables, coffee, tea and sugar. In the absence of potatoes, dried beans are useful. Flour is essential and also sugar.'[113]

Creating a list of requirements was one thing – and even that contained only the bare minimum – but accessing and delivering them brought its own set of difficulties. 'Food was a big problem,' remembered Joe Peloquin. But once again the initiative and cunning of the Resistance and the local families provided a solution, even if it meant going without food themselves and accompanied by the stark horrors of potentially being discovered.

A young girl, Micheline Fiuchard, would deliver bread daily to the camp on a horse-drawn cart from Fontaine-Raoul, a village 2 miles away from the forest (on one trip she was strafed by Allied aircraft as she travelled along the country roads). People from nearby towns and villages suddenly became enthusiastic night-time anglers, fishing from the banks of the River Loire out of sight of the Germans for carp and catfish which would then be smuggled into the camp. Local farmers provided whatever milk, butter and eggs they could spare.

Jonathan Pearson III, who had been shot down on 3 March and had been hiding in France for three months before finally making his way into the forest camp on 10 June with Yankus, recalled how 'French men and women brought us some supplies but we foraged by night and frequently even by day for meat, wine, poultry and vegetables, paying farmers for their produce.'

His comments suggest that small groups of evaders would regularly leave the forest to seek food and drink but, in reality, while they would occasionally forage at night within the confines of the forest for mushrooms, rabbits and even wild boar (which they never succeeded in catching), the only man venturing outside during the day to secure additional vegetables, meat and wine was Boussa, well stocked with money from the camp for such eventualities. This money was issued by Berry who, on the opening of the camp, had been given 5 million French francs by MI9 to cover the cost of provisions and extras required for the camp. With the camp in full swing however, his expenses quickly mounted. 'I paid out between twenty and twenty-four thousand francs each week,' he recalled.

Meat was generally obtained from local farms but one of the camp dwellers, Sergeant Marion Knight, who had been a cattle rancher before the war, was delegated by Berry to venture out at night to kill a sheep, pig or rabbit that he would butcher and give to Yankus, who had worked in kitchens in the USA before the war, to cook. Every time Knight ventured out – and it was always under cover of darkness – it had to be agreed because one of the main rules of the camp was that nobody should ever leave the forest. 'No one was allowed to leave camp unless for water or other fatigues or with special permission to collect food,' recalled Berry. It was strictly forbidden on security grounds. 'Everyone knew too much,' he added, 'and if caught and made to talk by the Gestapo's methods, the lives of the whole camp, as well as helpers and the Resistance, would be in danger. Everyone was warned they could be shot by the Resistance for breaking the rules and that I would report them, resulting in a court martial.'

Despite these rules, some in the camp felt it was their duty to try to return to Britain. Sergeant N.J. McCarthy detected an attitude amongst some of the evaders in the camp that 'the order they must NOT leave camp to reach our lines … was contrary to evasion training, which teaches an evader he should leave any organisation and reach our lines on his own if he feels the organisation is not doing sufficient for him in respect of getting home.' As it turned out, only one man broke this rule when he ventured to a local farm without permission. Not discovered by either the Germans or the Resistance he returned to the forest where he faced the wrath of Berry and was confined to camp for three weeks, a bizarre punishment given that all the men were, by nature, imprisoned within the camp anyway.

Local Resistance member Marcel Ridau was one of those who did what he could to bring food into the camp, but Flight Lieutenant Alex Campell remembered how their supplies for a while consisted of one particular food.

Our main diet consisted of apples, green apples. 1944 must have been a good year. They could be eaten in quite a number of ways and usually with the same effect especially when raw. We did have some rather pleasant diversions often brought in by our benefactors. One interesting thing was the making of ersatz coffee. Being harvest time, barley was becoming available in quantity. By rubbing it between your hands you could remove most of the chaff and by blowing on it you would be left with a few precious grains of barley. A source of heat was needed for our cooking and other such operations. From a recently abandoned dump a suitably sized chunk of steel plate was acquired. Resting on a few stone supports it provided an ideal cooking surface. The barley was spread out on the centre of the plate and carefully watched till it showed signs of being properly roasted. It was then brushed to the outer edges to be replaced by a fresh batch of barley. Using clear spring water, the freshly roasted grounds were brought to a boil in a tin can. Smaller tins and other makeshift containers were used as cups from which to sip the tasty coffee.

By now the camp had been divided into specific areas: the main communal area was named Piccadilly Circus, the area where any disciplinary action was taken became Hyde Park Corner and the kitchen was called Haymarket. Manned mainly by Yankus, the kitchen was a primitive affair where charcoal heated an 'oven' made from stones and corrugated iron. The charcoal was crucial as it gave out neither smoke nor smell and was provided by a local forest worker, Henri Lefèvre, who was connected to the Resistance.

In July, Ray Worrall finally made it into Fréteval Forest after being collected from the farm where he'd been hiding out under the supervision of a local family. 'So, we said goodbye to the family, thanked them for their hospitality of course, and said how thankful we were because the chances of being caught were very high and they'd have been shot, no doubt. And it was a long walk, and it shouldn't have been a long walk really, it should have just been a quarter of a mile over there but, in case anyone was watching, they took a detour. And then we came to the forest, and as we approached the forest they said, "Well, you're leaving us now, go into that wood." And so we thanked them for taking us there, and they turned around and went home and we walked into the forest.'

Worrall was not only shocked by what he found in the forest but by what was on offer to eat. 'We were surprised when we got into the forest that it was full of airmen. There were over a hundred airmen there at the time, but they were living terribly rough on the ground. It was a big forest area, actually but we only stayed in one part of it and there was at least a hundred airmen there then, and they were existing on very short rations. The Resistance, who we had contact with, brought food in for them at very great risk, not very much as they didn't have much themselves, so we had very little to eat. We got a little bit of coffee for breakfast and a piece of bread. At lunchtime, one or two turned themselves into cooks and we had a charcoal fire and boiled some water, there was a well nearby, so we got some water and they made a sort of stew with a few vegetables, so that was our lunch. Then it came to supper, which was a cup of this terrible tasting coffee and a piece of bread and butter. It wasn't a very substantial diet. But it was all we could have.'

One thing that all the Englishmen in the camp missed was their beloved tea. Despite the best efforts of the French Resistance, not a single ounce of tea was procured for them during their stay in the forest and even the future parachute drops neglected this most basic of English requirements.

Worrall's Australian bomb aimer, Murray, who had also made it to Fréteval, was equally shocked by the food. 'The food situation was acute. Occasionally a friendly farmer would bring a few vegetables or a leg of veal, and then we would have a royal feast. In the meantime, we had nothing but beans, and only one meal a day. The usual menu was two pieces of black bread for breakfast, beans for lunch, and two pieces of bread and a mug of ground barley coffee for supper. During the three weeks I was in camp I lost one stone in weight.'

Sometimes, very rarely, there was a welcome addition to the menu. Canadian Flight Lieutenant Campbell recalled a hot summer's day in the forest when a stranger was escorted into the camp by one of the sentries guarding the camp.

He was carrying a burlap sack which appeared to be heavily loaded. With a look of relief, he lowered it to the ground. Being on food detail that day I was one of several persons present at the time. The sack had dark red stains showing through from the inside. As the sack was opened a cluster of flies emerged circling and buzzing about. Peering inside we saw a number of dead rabbits in a variety of colours, shapes and sizes, seven in all. I suspect they were somebody's pets and had all met the same sacrifice. In a rather fortunate turn one of our number was rumoured to be an experienced cook. As it turned out he may not have been too experienced in food preparation, especially with dead rabbits. However, we all enjoyed a taste of rabbit stew that evening along with a surprise helping of peas. Now this fed some sixty young, forever-hungry fliers who seldom complained – it was unwise to do so.

De Blommaert managed to find some honey every so often to sweeten the spirits of the evaders, and they would occasionally have hot chocolate in the evenings by melting some Baker's chocolate in hot water but, overall, it was a poor diet and not particularly varied, a situation hardly helped by the basic cooking facilities. For eating implements, the early camp arrivals were issued with a fork, knife, spoon and mug, but as more evaders arrived the cutlery had to be shared.

If the food was now rudimentary and meagre with so many 'inmates', the sleeping conditions weren't much better with the men crammed three or four into the makeshift tents, between shifts on watch at the edges of the forest. To begin with the tents were essentially tarpaulins simply draped over cross-poles and fixed to trees. For bedding all each evader had was a blanket and two sacks. Although it was summer, this was barely enough to keep you warm at night, so some preferred doing a night-time sentry watch in four-hour shifts, then sleeping during the warmth of the day. As the numbers of evaders in the camp grew and provisions became scarce, the new arrivals had a choice: instead of a blanket and two sacks they had to choose whether they took the blanket *or* the two sacks. However, Pete Berry instigated the rough construction of a 'sawing horse', which meant that frames for elementary beds could be made as well as other wooden necessities.

Hygiene was another major issue. The natural spring in the camp enabled them to wash, shave, brush teeth and clean clothes, but they couldn't risk contaminating their water supply. Consequently, latrines were dug a distance away from the camp, consisting of no more than a ditch over which a bench roughly constructed from a tree trunk was laid allowing the evaders to sit down in relative comfort.

Perhaps, however, what the men missed more than anything was tobacco. Cigarettes were in great demand but in short supply. 'Morale on the whole was extremely good,' said Berry, 'although the shortage of cigarettes was the greatest difficulty.' Brayley recalled that when the situation was particularly bad, Resistance members would steal them from the local stores in Chartres. On one occasion, as Campbell remembered, a young girl entered the camp, with de Blommaert and Boussa, smoking a cigarette.

As rumours flourished quite a number of us gathered at the meeting place. She was in conversation with a small group of men, two of which were known to us. We learned that the third man was a Belgian and noticed that the girl spoke fluently with him and also with our two acquaintances although in different languages. Being unable to understand the conversation, let alone join in, we occupied our time discussing by what means we might be able to entertain this young lady. At one point, she discarded a partly used cigarette and stepped on it. Quite shamelessly a number of us made an attempt to salvage the prize. On seeing our reaction, she turned to us and said in clear, concise English, 'I have extra cigarettes, would you boys like some?' Our minds immediately recalled our recent comments about this young lady but, nonetheless, we graciously accepted her offer.

But despite the evaders having crude tents, the locals providing rationed food, drink and cigarettes and the Germans keeping their distance, there was one problem that was proving hard to tackle. And at MI9 Neave was all too aware of it. 'Boredom and anxiety were extremely difficult to combat,'[114] he wrote. Unless they were addressed – and quickly – they could threaten the very security of the camp.

CHAPTER 16

DAILY ROUTINE

Each day in the camp at Fréteval began at 6 am with Reveille. Immediately on waking the evaders would cover their tents with branches and foliage to ensure they couldn't be spotted from the sky. At ground level they were hidden from the roads and fields surrounding the forest by the thick undergrowth and sturdy tree trunks. What no one initially recognised, however, was the threat from the sky. Although the Allied air forces now started to rule the skies, there were frequent forays over the forest by German planes.

The basic tarpaulin tents couldn't be seen from the sky at night but during daylight they could be spotted from above. Consequently, camouflaging them every morning was essential. And, as Peloquin explained, they were equally worried they might be spotted by American planes who would also 'have shot us; they didn't know who we were or what side we were on'.

Next, charcoal fires would be lit to prepare breakfast and to heat water for washing. While some evaders were tasked with carrying water from the spring to the camp others cleaned up the site but, once the basic tasks had been done and the standard breakfast of coffee and a slice of bread eaten, the rest of the day offered very little to occupy the evaders. 'Boredom was the real enemy,' recalled Cliff Hallett, despite them being under the noses of the Germans and knowing they had to conduct themselves accordingly.

'It was amazing we weren't caught because we could see the German vehicles passing the road. I think they were almost within a stone's throw,' remembers Worrall. 'They were in cars, the typical Volkswagen cars. There was usually two in them with helmets on as they went past. So, we could hide behind the trees and see. It was quite frightening really, the whole thing was frightening to be honest. Everyday we expected to be caught and if we were caught we would have been executed because our uniform was taken off us at the farmhouse and we were given civilian clothing so we had no uniform protection.'

It was simply a question of making the best of a bad situation. Once a week the evaders would look forward to the visit of Albert Barillet, a trusted barber from the neighbouring village who would give them a shave and keep their hair cut to regulation length. A doctor also came but, other than these visits, human interaction with outsiders was kept to a minimum and any meetings with women were strictly off-limits. Occasionally the evaders would get a glimpse of the farmer's attractive daughter who fetched water at another well at the edge of the woods and, as Hallett recalled, 'On Sundays all eyes turned to the meadow where her sister looked after the sheep, which lifted the boredom. However, there was no direct contact with the fairer sex but plenty of talk about it.'

Many of the men would pass the time keeping fit and doing sits-ups, press-ups or using branches to support pull-ups. Sunbathing became a popular pastime in a clearing in the woods, but an improvised sign dictated that there would be 'No Sunbathing On Sundays'. The reason, according to Murray, was that 'the Germans took their girlfriends walking on Sundays and being caught with one's pants down was a thing that would not have been appreciated.' But whilst the weather in the forest was ideal for sunbathing it was also the perfect environment for plagues of unwanted visitors.

According to Worrall, 'It was pretty hot, and we'd had one or two thunderstorms, but the heat was terrific. There were wasp nests all over the place. You had to be very careful you didn't put your foot on one because they'd swarm around and could have been deadly. Of course, once you started to eat a bit of food the wasps would come around and you'd find one in your spoon and you'd have to be careful you didn't swallow it. It wasn't much fun.' Campbell also remembered the plague of insects. 'Wasps were everywhere, and one could zoom in at the last split second as you tried to ram in a spoonful full of apple sauce.

If you were lucky you could just spit it out before being stung. Snakes also appeared on the scene. I believe they were called vipers but I can't recall what they looked like. They must have been harmless as I don't remember hearing of anyone being bitten by them.'

To escape the heat – and sometimes the wasps – the evaders took advantage of the local spring. 'The brave ones would strip down and jump in. It really cooled you off,' recalled Campbell.[115]

Games provided more relief from the boredom. A rudimentary chess set was made from whatever could be found, and the evaders could often be found whittling away at sticks with their blunt knives. 'We could have started a good business in carved walking sticks after a few weeks,' recalled Murray. The Americans also fashioned a golf course that they christened the Fréteval Country Club and tournaments were organised. 'One or two people tried to make themselves golf "sticks" out of broken twigs,' Worrall said. 'Otherwise we just sat around and chatted amongst ourselves, telling each other about our experiences.'

These conversations were all conducted via whispers as the Germans continued to patrol the perimeters of the forest. Once or twice, gunfire was heard amongst the trees as German soldiers would venture into the forest on hunting trips. Immediately, upon hearing these gunshots the camp would assume silence and all fires would be extinguished, with the evaders lying low until any prospect of being discovered by the Germans had passed.

On another occasion, at night-time, a group of three

hundred German soldiers set up camp just four hundred yards from the forest as they made their way to counter the Allied advance on the Normandy front. Upon discovering the Germans were close by, Berry gave the order to extinguish all fires, not light anymore and that silence be adhered to all night until the Germans left the following morning. 'That night we had nothing to eat and couldn't speak,' recalled Hallett. 'It was quite terrifying. Boussa said that if anything happened it was every man for himself. This was particularly worrying for me because I was injured and still on a stretcher at that point. He said they wouldn't be able to carry me, so I would have to be left. The Germans would get me and all he asked was that I kept my trap shut for twenty-four hours to give everyone a chance to get as far away as possible. "Then you can tell them whatever you like," he said. It was a pretty nasty prospect, given what the Germans were capable of.'[116]

Card schools were another way to pass the time. Poker became the main game with the Americans confident they could beat the British. Before long, money was being played for and Hallett, a novice poker player before the war began, suddenly found himself beating all comers and within a few days had cleaned the rest of the evaders out of all their escape money. In all, Hallett had won some £600 and the other evaders, desperate to win their money back, approached Boussa for credit. Boussa, however, refused their demands for fear that gambling could put an end to the good atmosphere in the camp. It seemed a wise move at the time but, in fact, the generally amiable and decent atmosphere in the camp was already beginning to disintegrate.

One of the new entrants into the forest was US pilot Captain William Davis of 485 Fighter Squadron, who had finally reached Fréteval after being shot down during a mission to bomb targets in the Loire Valley.

I moved every day, staying in some new barn or field where Resistance members would bring me food. Their security seemed very good, though often they talked a lot. I was fed well, and the Frenchmen told me they had sent a message to London and that I had been identified as a result. These people were well organised. They had plenty of Sten guns and ammunition and a British radio. There had been several parachute operations in that region [near Châteaudun]. I was told that a big camp for evaders and escapers had been established near where I was, and that I would be taken to it when one of the men in charge had come to see me. But when I went there I was shocked by what I saw.

I went first to the part of the camp run by F/Lt Berry. Discipline did not seem very good and there was a lot of bitching going on. The ranking British officers tried hard but did not seem able to control the men. A lot of them were drunk every night on calvados or cognac, and several wandered off to the farms and towns around the forest. The head agent [Boussa] made too many impossible promises. I do not think he had ever done such work before, and he did not understand the psychology of a bunch of men living together under these conditions at all. In this part of the camp nobody did any work if they could help it.

There is no evidence to support Davis's claims that drunk evaders wandered out of the camp and into neighbouring communities, but it does appear that a rift was beginning to develop, especially between the British and the Americans, a rift that could possibly split the camp, lead to a major dispute and potentially to the camp being discovered.

Worrall observed it developing and realised quickly how catastrophic it threatened to become. 'I was open-minded about what was going to happen. At least I was still alive, that was my first thought. And with people I know. But it wasn't just the RAF: there were Canadians, Australians and a lot of American airmen. And they knew better than anyone they were going to win the war, so there was a lot of trouble and Lucien got very worried with the Americans as they used to say, "Goddam it, we're going to be shot as dead ducks here, let's get away." Of course, Lucien said, "You don't get away. If you try to get away, and the Germans don't find you and shoot you, we'll do it because once someone's caught the game's up." The Americans were causing trouble amongst ourselves and a lot of the other chaps who were Canadians, Australians and so on, and you know how the American talks, it was getting people's backs up terribly. It was a terribly dangerous situation.'

Hallett also remembered the growing discontent between the British and the Americans. 'The English had had enough of the showing off of their transatlantic cousins. As far as they were concerned everything in America was twice as big, twice as good, twice as nice as in England. They naively stated that in actual fact only they could win the war. They did not want to hear that they had not wanted to know about the events in Europe 'til Pearl Harbor and Hitler's declaration of war forced them to take up arms.'

Friction between British and American servicemen had been bubbling away ever since the first American troops had landed in Britain in 1942, a time when British morale was low following the setbacks of the North African and Far East campaigns. The Americans arriving on British shores were well paid, wore smart modern uniforms and enjoyed a significantly better quality (and, perhaps more importantly, quantity) of food. In addition, their equipment seemed better and they had more money, which they were all to keen to flash about. This created resentment amongst the British troops, especially those serving overseas who were anxious that the GIs were fraternising with their women back home and they lived in fear of receiving the dreaded 'Dear John' letter. (By October 1942, nearly two thousand men fighting in the Middle East had divorce cases underway, some undoubtedly caused by the Americans.)

Conversely, the American soldiers disliked the British officers' politeness, which they saw as a distraction from honest discussion; the cultural, social and military differences appeared almost insurmountable.

But once the British and Americans began working together the relationship improved dramatically, and in the autumn of 1943 a scheme was introduced with American and British troops embedded in each other's units. Initiated by the authorities, the scheme was inspired by the experience of the armies in North Africa. It was the first location where the two armies had actually fought together, and the initial suspicion and rivalry quickly gave way to respect once the Yanks had been blooded in combat. One American soldier summed it up: 'When I was back in England I didn't have such a good impression of the English but when you fight with them, and next to them, they are really all right.'[117]

However, being cooped up together in a primitive camp in a forest directly under the noses of the enemy, unarmed, detached, exhausted, living on meagre rations and with little to pass the time of day, tensions and conflicts were bound to arise in what was, effectively, enforced captivity. 'It was a prison, yes it was a prison,' suggests Worrall.

Berry did what he could to diffuse any situations. Right from the start he offered any evader the right to call a meeting of the camp at any point to air grievances. He named it a 'Bitch Session' and here an evader could 'state his case, complain or criticise without future prejudice whether it was against an officer or not, including myself', he said. Following a complaint the camp would then vote on a new ruling unless, in the opinion of Berry, it was prejudicial to the wellbeing or safety of the camp. According to Berry's testimony, these sessions were held weekly and, with just a few exceptions, were on small matters of policy and minor complaints.

Back in London at Room 900 of MI9, Neave was

oblivious to much of this. Despite the intricate planning, he was having trouble receiving radio communication from those running the camp, especially de Blommaert. His radio operator had remained in Paris to work with the remnants of the Comet Line and, consequently, Neave only had intermittent contact with him. The other radio operator, Toussaint, who was detailed to Boussa, was operating from outside the camp and had to change his place of operation frequently to avoid detection by the Germans. Moreover, he had left his spare radio and set of crystals at Bayonne with members of the Comet Line. (At the end of the war it emerged that the Comet Line had actually sent the spare set to Toussaint by train to Paris but it was destroyed when the train carrying it from Paris to Châteaudun was hit by a bomb). The upshot was that neither de Blommaert nor Boussa could be confident that any of their transmissions were reaching London and, likewise, Neave couldn't be sure that his messages were being received. He was well aware that this could have far-reaching effects on the camp. 'Had there been better radio contact, I should certainly have been able to send more supplies to him [Boussa]. The sick and wounded suffered in consequence, despite the devotion of their French helpers.'[118] Meanwhile Boussa had been trying to get messages through to London to drop fresh supplies having found a nearby drop zone, but each night he reported to the camp that he had failed to get through to London.

Morale dropped accordingly but it was eventually tempered by the fact that a radio receiver had finally been secured that provided a window on the state of the war in Britain and Europe. 'Most evenings we would be summoned down to the meeting place for a brief gathering round a very subdued and smokeless fire,' recalled Campbell. 'We were often handed a piece of heavy, unsweetened, dark rye bread. We could take turns beside the bed of hot coals and make toast. If there was no coffee that night we could always drink spring water. Another luxury was the delicious smell of hot chocolate. This was made by melting lumps of hard Baker's chocolate in hot water. While enjoying our bedtime treat we could listen to the BBC news and often the Vichy version as well. On comparing the two reports, we could come up with a fairly accurate picture of the progress of the approaching Allied Forces.'

Unfortunately for them, however, the news only highlighted the fact that the Allies' hopes for a rapid advance following the D-Day landings had been dashed. While the Allies were clinging on to their foothold in France and had established a firm beachhead, the Germans were offering stiff resistance farther inland and there was no sign of the anticipated rout. General Montgomery's Second Army had planned to take Caen by midnight on D-Day, thereby opening a way into France but, having second-guessed Monty, the German commanders ensured the city was heavily defended and had placed a Panzer division on the high ground in front of the city. While the odds facing the Germans were impossible – they could never hope to win a major victory – they could significantly slow down the Allies and inflict major casualties. Ultimately, Monty was unsuccessful in his efforts to take Caen by midnight and it was added to the list of Normandy locations targeted by Bomber Command. It would be two months before Caen was in Allied hands, by which time 73% of the city had been reduced to rubble and thousands of civilians had been killed.

Monty wasn't the only commander struggling to make headway through France. The city of Bayeux had not been taken as planned and none of the invasion forces had reached their Day One objectives. The Desert Rats were also making slow progress because of the sunken lanes and high hedges of Normandy. Their Cromwell tanks were more used to the terrain of North Africa but here, with hedgerows at least three times the height of English ones, the enemy were frequently out of sight and just a week after D-Day the Desert Rats were halted by an ambush of German Tiger tanks outside the town of Villers-Bocage. One by one, every Cromwell tank was destroyed by the superior German machines and the British forces withdrew into defensive positions.

Elsewhere, instead of pushing forward, the Allied front line was simply becoming a logjam as troops that should have been moving forward aggressively dug in. Only two weeks after D-Day, the Allies' progress was flagging and when the weather changed for the worse in Normandy in June they were forced to cancel air operations, which gave the Germans time to reinforce their Normandy defences. Nevertheless, by 12 June the Allies held a front that was 60 miles long and 15 miles deep into Normandy, and 160,000 troops had crossed the English Channel. The desperate war in Normandy would last for another three months with almost half a million casualties on both sides as the Allies endeavoured to break out from the beachhead and head inland.

Listening on the radio and hearing news brought into the camp by Boussa, the evaders in Fréteval were aware that the invasion had taken place and that the Allies were now only 150 miles away. But how long they would take to reach the camp and liberate them nobody knew. The evaders had been in the camp for a short time but the number hidden there had grown considerably and tensions were rising in an environment of fear, uncertainty and deprivation. There were simply too many of them to exist safely, securely and happily side by side. With no indication when they might be liberated, there was only one course of action to take; create another camp in the forest. And again, right under the noses of the Germans.

CHAPTER 17

THE SECOND CAMP

By the middle of June, the number of men in the camp had risen to seventy with the prospect of more evaders being brought in daily over the coming weeks. There were only twenty-five makeshift tents to share between them all and the atmosphere was becoming increasingly strained and untenable. 'When the numbers reached seventy I decided the camp was not large enough and a larger number together would be dangerous,' decided Berry. He met de Blommaert, Boussa and Lake to discuss the situation and propose the new camp.

The tension between the British and the Americans was beginning to increase again, although some of the Americans thought Boussa was the main problem, not Berry. US airman Donald Lewis was in Fréteval for two months during which time he 'formed a definite opinion that Lucien was a bungler. He lacked energy and initiative and did not seem to be the man for the job. This was the opinion of most of the others in the camp.'

Peloquin recalled an unsavoury moment when tensions between Boussa and de Blommaert almost reached boiling point right in front of everyone. 'I remember that Lucien and Jean had an argument. I suppose that both wanted to be number one man, plus we were getting too big for the area.' Berry, however, was ambivalent about Boussa's role. 'He was excellent in all he did for the camp on the outside but was less successful when he interfered within the camp. He did not understand the British mentality, and his excitable way upset the men. He had trouble with his radio operator,* whom he distrusted. Unfortunately, he told this to the camp, which affected morale and caused uneasiness.'

De Blommaert, Lake and Boussa all agreed with Berry's proposal for a second camp and it was Jubault who, with his extensive knowledge of the forest, came up with a potential location. He suggested a spot on the southern edge of the forest at a place called Richery, approximately four miles from the current camp. It had both a stream and a small lake, and Jubault knew it well having considered it as a hiding place during his time on the run. It was ideal he thought, although it was in closer proximity to a number of heavily guarded German ammunition dumps.

---

* This is not a reference to Francois Toussaint who was a dependable and trustworthy member of the operation, but instead refers to a local French radio operator whom Boussa had recruited in a vain attempt to get messages to MI9. This operator claimed to have been trained in England but had lost touch with his organisers. However, he also failed to make regular contact with Room 900.

THE SECOND CAMP

'De Blommaert considered that the presence of German guards was an advantage since it kept away the curious and the enemy would never suspect his choice of hiding place,' wrote Neave.[119]

Over the next few days it was prepared for occupation and on 25 June 1944 the first ten evaders, all Americans, bid Berry and the others goodbye and trekked across the forest to the new camp, imaginatively named Camp 2. The original camp would now assume the equally imaginative name of Camp 1. Berry had put First Lieutenant Geno di Betta in charge of Camp 2. Di Betta had been Berry's second-in-command in Camp 1 and had acquitted himself well. Also in his favour was his nationality; he was an American and Camp 2 was going to be almost exclusively American. Straight away morale appeared to be better in this new camp. The Americans immediately set about creating a golf course and would creep out at night to gather straw for their beds from nearby farms.

While Boussa, perhaps with his tail slightly between his legs, remained with the British and other nationalities at Camp 1, de Blommaert moved into Camp 2 and helped to run it as well as organising the delivery of supplies from local farmers, civilians and Resistance members. 'I went to Camp 2 later on,' recalled Joe Peloquin, 'and Jean [de Blommaert] now was number-one man there. That made him happier.'

One of the first evaders into Camp 2 was William Davis (of 485 Fighter Squadron) and he recalled the influence de Blommaert had on this camp. 'If anyone deserves credit for the success of the whole scheme it is he. He held the men together for nine weeks by the force of his example and by his unusual understanding of their needs and characters. He lived with them throughout, unlike the other Belgian agent [Boussa] who supplied us with money. I hope he is suitably rewarded. He was quite fearless and used to go out and investigate when any Germans were nearby. Once he was picked up by the Germans but bluffed his way out by pretending to be a Belgian worker from a nearby town. He helped maintain security – no easy job – as the Germans had an ammunition dump only 400 yards away.'

Despite its close proximity to Camp 1, at no time during their stay in the forest was the location of Camp 2 revealed to any of the men in Camp 1. However, all new evaders who would end up in Camp 2 were first brought to Camp 1 to be interrogated by Boussa and Berry.

On 4 July a group of Americans from Camp 2 were walking through the forest foraging for food. Amongst them was Brayley. Despite the help of the locals, their food rations were still meagre but on this particular day they found something that made them forget about food for a short while. They stumbled across a flask in the undergrowth. Opening it they were thrilled to discover it contained alcohol and, being Americans on 4 July, they stopped to toast Independence Day.

It wasn't long before Camp 2 had also acquired a radio, enabling them to listen to news of the Allied advance, which was now picking up speed. Any important information that was heard over the radio was written down and pinned on a tree to act as a bulletin board. Each night they would listen out for the phrase 'Don't wait on the star', the coded signal from London broadcast over the BBC, which meant there would be a parachute drop that night. It meant much-needed fresh supplies and provisions.

The local Resistance was doing what it could to keep both camps reasonably well supplied with food and the occasional alcoholic drink, but as ever cigarettes and chocolate were what the evaders really desired. 'Cigarettes were the most essential requirement,' recalled Berry, 'as without them morale drops immediately. Chocolate is second best for keeping up morale.'

Back at MI9 in London, Neave was conscious that he needed to keep the evaders' spirits up – as well as looking after their physical and mental welfare – and that this could really only be achieved by parachute drops of provisions. One of the reasons Fréteval had been chosen was its proximity to areas ideal for such drops. Early on, Neave was aware that there were not enough tents to shelter the men and set about organising a parachute drop in late June. These drops needed to be carefully co-ordinated.

When the signal came through from Britain, three men from the Resistance would head to the drop zone and, when the aircraft was about to approach, form a triangle in the open field. Carrying red flashlights to indicate to the pilot the direction of the wind on the ground, they would be visible to the approaching aircraft that would parachute the metal containers in. It was a risky operation for those guiding the aircraft in: at any point they could be discovered by the enemy, their red flashlights proving as much a beacon to the German night patrols as to the incoming aircraft.

On this June night, the evaders were full of excitement having heard the coded message. This would be the first parachute drop and it wasn't only the prospect of supplies that excited them but confirmation that the operational structure put in place for the parachute drops would work. Murray, in Camp 1, remembered this night well. 'The night the aircraft was due every man in both camps was out listening. About 1 am we heard it coming. A Halifax flying at about five hundred feet. We all muttered a kind of prayer, because we knew there was an ack-ack battery only a few miles away. The aircraft thundered overhead towards the drop zone. The next morning, we awaited the arrival of the chief with great anticipation. He was a little later than usual and he did not look very happy when he did come. Our hearts sank when he told us the aircraft had gone to the wrong field. As there were no recognition signals, it had returned to base with its precious cargo.'

It was a crushing blow. 'When a drop failed to materialise, morale dropped low. On one occasion, a plane made several passes over the area, then went off without dropping supplies. The men felt very low,' recalled Brayley. Nobody knew why the drop had failed, they could only speculate and blame was hastily laid at everyone's door, such was the desperation for fresh supplies and, also, a link, however tenuous, with those back home, a feeling that they weren't forgotten. The failed drop was also a huge blow to Neave who later wrote, 'Owing to a misunderstanding, the aircraft returned without dropping its load. For some reason, de Blommaert did not receive the message until too late and there was no reception.'[120]

Undeterred, Neave tried again during the first week in July in an operation named Jupiter. During the night of 6/7 July, similar plans were put into operation, this time using a different field for the drop in case the Germans had intercepted the plans for the previous aborted drop and were lying in wait. Brayley's entry for 7 July described what happened. 'Beautiful black Halifax bomber roars over our heads. Bomb doors open, fifteen white parachutes drop out and swing like pendulums over the wheat field. We run for the containers. We work feverishly until dawn.' Neave had sent over stoves, plates, saucepans, tents, rations, medical supplies, more French francs, cigarettes and chocolate amongst other items, some useful, some not so much. 'The camp then received one packet of 24-hour rations, 200 packets of cigarettes, razors but no blades and delousing powder which was not necessary,' added Berry.

Determined to ensure the parachute left no trace, de Blommaert's helpers in the French Resistance went out into the wheat fields at first light to restore the wheat, which had been flattened by the containers, back into the upright position.

In the camps, everyone was delighted. In his 8 July diary entry Brayley wrote, 'Clothing doled out. We have a joke.

If it fits, bring it back' and two days later, on July 10, he wrote, 'We make blankets out of parachutes. Embroidery classes start with the thread from parachute cables. New talent discovered.'

As well as tents, chocolate, clothing and cigarettes (Gauloises, of course, for if any empty packets of Players or Gold Flake had been blown away and found by the Germans they might well get discovered), one of the most important contents of the containers parachuted in was medicine. With the camps now housing over one hundred evaders, split between the British, Canadians, Aussies and other nationalities in Camp 1 and the Americans being the sole occupiers of Camp 2, the number of sick and injured was also rising as wounded aircrew were brought in by the Resistance. Most suffered superficial wounds such as cuts and burns sustained when parachuting out of their burning aircraft but, occasionally, they were significantly worse.

Hallett had received internal injuries when baling out of his plane as well as severe cuts to his legs when he crawled out of the wheat fields to avoid detection by German patrols. He had been placed on a special diet during a visit to the camp by a local doctor, Dr Teyssier from Cloyes, who would arrive weekly to check up on the evaders or be summoned to the forest if there was a medical emergency. As well as the visits from Dr Teyssier, a male nurse was appointed within the camp from amongst the evaders. His duty was to specifically look after the ill and wounded who had been placed within an 'ambulance tent'. In the Jupiter parachute drop in early July, Airey Neave had sent drugs and medicines as well as D.D.T. to help disinfect the straw used within the beds that the evaders were sleeping on.* Within the 'ambulance tent' the mildly sick and wounded were cared for by evaders who had basic medical skills, using the medicine parachuted in or secured by the Resistance. Any evaders with more serious wounds or symptoms were, upon inspection by Dr Teyssier, moved to and hidden in a house on the edge of the forest belonging to an eighty-year-old French widow with a perfect command of English, Madame Despres, who, according to Jubault, was 'very alert for her age'.

Moving the sick airmen to her home, even though it was on the edge of the forest (it was just under seven miles away from Camp 1), was a dangerous and slow operation. Often the wounded had to be carried on a makeshift stretcher by Resistance operatives, which wasn't the easiest of tasks at night given the thick brush of the forest, and they also had to navigate the fifteen-minute patrols carried out by the Germans on the edge of the forest. The person responsible for moving the sick was Omer's sixteen-year-old daughter Ginette, who was often accompanied by her brother, Jean. Together, with little concern for their own safety, these two would lead the Resistance workers and the patient through the darkness to the home of Madame Despres. Before long,

---

* DDT (dichloro-diphenyl-trichloroethane) was developed as the first of the modern synthetic insecticides in the 1940s. It was initially used with great effect to combat malaria, typhus, and the other insect-borne human diseases among both military and civilian populations. Promoted as a wonder chemical after World War II, it has since been banned for agricultural uses worldwide following studies that have shown it to cause a number of health defects in humans such as breast & other cancers, male infertility, developmental delay, nervous system and liver damage and miscarriages amongst others.

her house had become a temporary sick bay, often with at least five evaders recuperating there at any one time.

Teyssier would frequently visit them, using rationed medicine from his own surgery or supplies that had been dropped by the Allies. Campbell recalled one incident when 'a helper escorted into our camp a young man whose face was swathed in what appeared to be curtain cloth. As we became more closely acquainted in the next few hours it was soon obvious he urgently needed medical attention. The colour and foul odour of the flesh verified the need for action. Somehow arrangements were made and with the ever-present risk of discovery the unnamed helpers managed to get the necessary medical help.'

General sickness, isolated bouts of sunstroke, wasp stings and the occasional laceration from branches were also treated by Teyssier, as were cases of lice, an inevitable consequence of the evaders wearing the same clothes for months on end without washing them. 'The washing of clothes was quite out of the question,' said Worrall, 'and we lived for weeks, some for nearly three months, in the same clothes, night and day.'

Second Lieutenant Robert D. Couture of 354 Fighter Squadron recalled falling ill in the camp. 'I was first taken in by the Marcel Roussea family at their farm outside Vichères. After a few days I moved on to the Houpillart home, where I received medical attention by Madame Houpillart. I was next moved by the Underground to Fréteval with six other airmen. Each day the Underground brought in more evaders. While in the forest my wounds became badly infected and I was taken to Madame Despres's château to receive medical attention. I remained there for four weeks and then returned to the forest.'

Like most of the others, Couture's wounds required simple treatment. However, on two occasions, Teyssier had to treat more serious medical conditions, as Brayley noted in his diary on 9 August. 'Shorty Craig gets appendicitis.' The evaders knew he needed to get attention immediately. They couldn't risk his appendix bursting and it turning into a full-scale medical emergency. But at the same time there was no possibility of him being operated on in the forest safely and by taking him to a nearby hospital, even one which would clandestinely admit such patients, there was no guarantee he'd be safe from discovery by the Germans. And if he was discovered by the Germans, the potential always existed that he would talk if 'encouraged' and give away their location. The only option they had was to take him to the home of Madame Despres where he could be treated by Teyssier. 'We dressed him up and carried him away,' wrote Brayley, and Craig was carried urgently through the forest and out into the open. Such was his pain and the potential seriousness of his condition that the evaders even risked moving him during daylight hours. They had no choice. It was life or death. Had they left him any longer the Germans might have heard his groans.

Confident the coast was clear, they left the forest, crossed the road and sank into the fields of wheat. They had no time to lift up their path of trodden wheat. Dodging between roads, paths and fields, stooping below hedgerows with back-breaking effort, they eventually made their way to the home of Madame Despres. They hadn't been spotted or followed. Teyssier was waiting for them with his son Louis. Neither were surgeons, but in war desperate times meant desperate measures. The fact that Teyssier was there at all was down to the efforts of de Blommaert.

Realising the seriousness of the situation, and with no imminent visit to the camp by the doctor, de Blommaert had taken it upon himself to walk the 10 miles to his surgery and fetch him while the casualty was being conveyed through the fields. And because it was pouring with rain, the journey was filled with even more risk because German soldiers could be taking cover under trees, beneath camouflaged canopies or huddled into hedgerows. They wouldn't be obvious, whereas a lone traveller making his way along roads and through fields would stand out. The stretcher-bearers faced the same problem. Now, with make-do instruments and little in the way of anaesthetic, Craig was operated on successfully and following a period of recuperation made his way back to the forest camp.

If the case of Shorty Craig was serious, the curious incident of Flight Sergeant Frank Wells, the rear gunner on Worrall's doomed Lancaster bomber, was more bizarre. Worrall and Wells had been separated following the attack on their plane that saw all the crew, bar one, bale out safely over France. With each man for himself on the ground, the two of them went their separate ways, both being picked up by different cells in the Resistance. Incredibly, just a few weeks later, virtually the entire crew of Worrall's

Lancaster found themselves reunited in Fréteval Forest. But when Frank Wells was brought in all was not well. He had suffered a gunshot wound to the ankle and needed urgent medical assistance. Dr Teyssier was called.

Wells was urgently conveyed to the makeshift hospital at the home of Madame Despres, where his leg was put in a plaster. Only when Wells returned to the forest following a period of recuperation, still plastered, did the events surrounding his injury come to light and, much to the amusement of the other evaders in the forest, it wasn't caused by the enemy. 'We weren't supposed to take firearms with us when we went on flying operations,' said Worrall, 'but Wells talked one of the WAFS in the armoury to giving him a pistol, a very good pistol actually, a Luger, arguing "If I'm shot down I want to be armed." He collected it every night before we went out.

'Wells was picked up by someone from the Resistance and was being brought to the forest, when they sat in a field for a rest. Now, this Frenchman had a grotty old revolver, it was all the protection he had, but Frank had this beautiful Luger and was showing it to this Frenchman and, you won't believe it, but Frank had left the safety catch off and he shot himself through the ankle.'

Returning to camp, Wells found that morale continued to remain low, especially in Camp 1 where Boussa was attracting more criticism. This wasn't helped by Boussa telling the evaders that they would be free by 15 July. Suddenly spirits rose, an end to their forced captivity was in sight, the prospect of returning home on the horizon. Of course, when 15 July passed without any sign of liberation, Boussa's stock fell even further. According to Berry, men within the camp 'ceased to believe' Boussa any more.

It didn't help that Boussa wasn't living in the camp. While the evaders existed as best they could under the trees, he spent much of his time and certainly his nights at the isolated home of Hallouin and his wife on the edge of the forest. Sergeant McCarthy was one of the evaders who clearly felt that Boussa might have been respected more had he roughed it out in the forest and 'seen the conditions and requirements at first hand instead of delegating this to Berry, the camp commander, who was an evader.' By not staying in the camp, McCarthy reasoned that Boussa failed to grasp or understand the mental attitude of the men in the camp, which resulted in 'a misunderstanding towards Boussa'.

Camp 1 was a far cry from Camp 2, where the Americans' morale remained high. They had fashioned their 'golf course' by now and were playing golf tournaments to stave off boredom. The friction with the British had disappeared now that they were no longer locked together. And, of course, it was being run by de Blommaert who seemed to have a better relationship with the evaders in his camp than Boussa did in his. Donald M. Lewis, who was in Camp 2, recalled de Blommaert as being '100 per cent better than Boussa and respected by all'. In fact, back at Camp 1 it wasn't just Boussa who was losing respect. Berry, the man originally put in charge of the whole camp by de Blommaert, was no longer universally popular.

THE SECOND CAMP

It was becoming obvious to some that Berry, before the war a tobacconist and only put in charge because he was the senior ranking officer, was simply not up to the job. Around him were young men, caged lions, all desperate to get home, all with a different take on life than Berry and few having much in common with him. One of the evaders reported that Berry had 'little idea of organisation of such a camp or of handling the men, especially under those conditions', before adding that 'stricter control was necessary. Berry aired his personal views, and, having no family ties had no understanding for those who had and were worrying … and he gave me the impression of having little interest in the camp or personnel. I believe that as a result the majority had no confidence in him, or any feeling of approach.'[121]

Whether Berry ever knew of the resentment towards him is impossible to say, but praise for him in the files of interviews provided by the evaders in his camp is scant. Matters were contained though because they were military men, trained to accept order, discipline and rank. And this they did, regardless of their feelings towards Berry and Boussa. That is testament itself to both the selection process and the rigorous training of the airmen by the RAF and one of the reasons why the camp at Fréteval remained undiscovered.

By the middle of July, while the British in Camp 1 sweated and stewed under the summer sun and the Americans in Camp 2 continued to make the best of their situation, news had filtered through that the invasion had taken place in Normandy and the hope was that the Allies would soon be at the edges of the forest to liberate the evaders. However, Boussa's claims that they would be free by 15 July had long passed without any sign of liberation and both camps were beginning to get twitchy. Nobody had any idea how long they would have to stay in the forest, and there was always the fear that the Germans would burst in as they retreated. Some evaders openly discussed the prospect of making a run for it, of chancing their arm out in the open. De Blommaert, Boussa and Berry put an end to such talk, but they all knew the men were living on the edge and that the sooner liberation came the better. In the meantime, they would just have to tough it out as best they could.

But events were about to happen that would test the mental and physical fortitude of even the hardest of men within both camps as a series of mishaps, close-shaves and bungled operations almost led to Operation Sherwood ending in disaster. Such were these sudden turns of events that it caused Brayley to write in his diary, 'The Siege of Fréteval is on and the Jerries begin a wave of terror.'

CHAPTER 18

CLOSING IN

It was 18 July 1944. While parachute drops specifically for the evaders at Fréteval were minimal (with only the Jupiter drop on 6/7 July being successful), regular parachute drops of arms and ammunition continued in the area for the Resistance.

The Resistance had played a vital role in the immediate aftermath of D-Day, undertaking nearly one thousand acts of sabotage by inflicting damage on railroads, ammunition dumps, fuel installations and communications networks, helping impede the flow of German reinforcements from arriving quickly in northern France. 'Without their great assistance the liberation of France and the defeat of the enemy in Western Europe would have consumed a much longer time and meant greater losses to ourselves,' remembered Eisenhower.

In the weeks following D-Day, the Resistance didn't let up

in their efforts to harass and disrupt the Germans, and their methods became increasingly confident and daring. Often this came at a terrible price, with the Germans torching towns and executing randomly selected French males in reprisals following Resistance raids. One such example was the massacre at Tulle on 9 June. The previous days had seen the local Resistance movement launch a successful offensive to support the D-Day landings and they had killed or wounded a significant number of German soldiers in and around the French town.* On 8 June, tanks from the 2nd SS Panzer Division swept into the area surprising the Resistance, retaking the town and causing the Resistance fighters to flee to the hills to regroup. The following day mass arrests were made in the town with all males between the ages of sixteen and sixty detained. From them 120 were selected for execution by hanging, their fate being announced on posters in the town. 'Forty German soldiers were murdered by the guerrillas, one hundred and twenty guerrillas and their accomplices will be hanged. Their bodies will be thrown in the river.'[122]

In groups of up to ten, the men of Tulle were led to their fate while the spokesperson for the Wehrmacht, Paula Geissler – known as 'the Bitch' – and a group of SS men watched as they downed wine on the terrace of the Café Tivoli and listened to music on a gramophone. Not all 120 were executed. The executions stopped at ninety-nine, but those spared that fate were transported, along with many others from Tulle, to Dachau concentration camp.

---

* Sarah Farmer, in her *Martyred Village* (University of California Press, 2000), estimates that 37 were killed, 25 wounded and 35 missing while Guy Penaud in *La 'Das Reich': 2e Panzer-Division* (La Lauze Editions, 2005) suggests that there was about 50 dead, 60 missing and from 25 to 37 wounded.

CLOSING IN

Despite such atrocities, the Germans failed to blunt the effectiveness and determination of the Resistance. Such was their nuisance that the crack 2nd SS Panzer Division, *Das Reich*, the division responsible for the massacres in Tulle and Oradour-sur-Glane, was diverted to anti-guerrilla operations in the Dordogne instead of being rushed to Normandy. If *Das Reich* had reached the Normandy battle in mid-June when the beachhead was at its most vulnerable, instead of trying to mop up insurgents of the Resistance, it is possible the Allies might have been thrown back into the English Channel and the path of Operation Overlord could have taken a different course.

Despite their successes, however, the efforts of the Resistance in the immediate weeks following D-Day were punctuated by periods of pandemonium. They were not trained soldiers and they were confronting a heavily armed military machine. The excitement of the D-Day landings had led to local Resistance groups embarking on operations with little planning and rarely any logistical organisation or co-operation with neighbouring groups. They got carried away by the prospect of an impending victory which, ultimately, led to the needless deaths of many Resistance members and the executions of civilians in acts of German reprisals.

Despite their haphazard operations, though, the Resistance made a sizeable contribution to the successful aftermath of D-Day, but in order to continue harassing the Germans and damaging the communications and transport infrastructure that the Germans relied on, they needed not only arms and ammunition but leadership. So the British created a crack team of operatives, initiated by the Special Operation Executive (SOE) and the Office of Strategic Services (OSS). At the beginning of 1944 this team, now codenamed Jedburgh by Colonel Wilkinson of SOE, was established at the Special Forces HQ in Baker Street, London. The aim was to parachute them into France, make contact with the Resistance, establish a communications network, supply weapons and ammunition, train people to use them and then harass and hinder the Germans. They were also ordered to take command of local Resistance units and act as a liaison between the Allied military and Resistance fighters.

Each three-man team (two officers and a wireless operator) would have either a British or American officer in charge with a French, Belgian or Dutch officer alongside. The first team parachuted into France on the eve of D-Day, being met by a reception committee from the Resistance group at Châteauroux. By the end of the first day of the Allied invasion, nearly three hundred young Allied soldiers had been dropped behind enemy lines to launch the secret Jedburgh sabotage missions with the Resistance.

No Jedburgh missions were dropped near Fréteval. What the Resistance movement there needed wasn't leadership (although that's debatable), but arms, ammunition and supplies. All around the forest suitable areas had been found for parachute drops. The evaders in the forest had been aware of aircraft passing overhead at night, hearing them as they dropped weapons, radios and francs for the Resistance, whereupon the arms and ammunition would be stored in nearby houses and farm outbuildings until required.

It was an odd emotion for the evaders, hearing these aircraft passing overhead, hoping they would be delivering supplies for them but learning the following day, when none were brought into the camps, that the drops were for the Resistance. These routine drops had been going without incident in the Fréteval region for a number of months, despite the fact that only one drop had been successfully undertaken for the evaders. However, on the night of 18 July everything changed.

A parachute drop had been planned for that night with arms and ammunition being sent for the Resistance. The weather forecast for the following two days was unsettled with fog and heavy rain threatening, so it was crucial that the parachute drop happened then despite the fact that the moon was waning and there wouldn't be another full moon until 4 August. Hearing an arranged coded message from the BBC at 7.30 pm on 18 July, the Resistance knew that a drop was on the way.

Back in England the aircrew responsible for the drop attended their briefing – their navigators and radio operators having already received their specialised orders in a separate briefing – before, at the appointed time, donning their flight gear and driving to their aircraft. Shortly after they were rumbling down the runway and taking off into darkness. Crossing over the Channel into France the crew looked out for the red lights indicating the drop zone on the ground. They expected the Resistance to be preparing trucks, carts, horses and any means of transport to whisk the containers away from the area before Germans arrived. Approaching the zone the aircraft dropped to 1,500 feet then 1,000 feet and, for the final approach, 500 feet. It was an exhilarating moment, even for the most experienced flyer, despite the chance that they could be shot down by a machine-gun at such a height. One airman, American Richard Goff, just nineteen years old, recalled his first breath-taking approach to the drop zone. 'We saw all the Resistance on the ground shouting and waving their arms in the air, we could even hear them! A chill went down my spine. It was great to think that these were our allies and not our enemy. I was just a lad amongst others, but I felt indestructible! I will remember that day for the rest of my life, it was the most fantastic mission I ever made.'

On this occasion, the aircraft dropped its containers and rapidly gained height to escape, before heading back to Britain. As it disappeared into the night, the Resistance began dragging the containers and their contents out of sight and loading them onto whatever transport was available to get them to an area of concealment before being moved on to Saint-Hilaire-la-Gravelle. But on this drop the Resistance made an error. The operatives, perhaps not as well trained as others, or possibly over-excited, were clumsy when covering up evidence of the drop. With the wheat fields yet to be harvested, the paths of the Resistance were plainly obvious because they failed to cover their tracks by brushing the wheat upright. This was a well-worn discipline that the Resistance invariably adhered to at all times. Except on this occasion.

Not only did the trampled wheat provide evidence of the drop, it also presented the Germans, who were quickly on the scene, with paths leading direct to the hiding places of the Resistance and to the farms where the arms and ammunition were hidden. Most of the Resistance fled as the Germans closed in on them, but amongst those apprehended was a local farm worker, Maxime Plateau. He was taken away for interrogation. The Germans knew the weapons were for the Resistance and had been aware of the parachute drops for some time, but they seemed to know nothing of the two camps in Fréteval Forest. The problem was that Plateau was all too aware of the camps; he was one of the main suppliers of food to the evaders, and now he faced the terrifying prospect of torture.

When news filtered through into the camps that Plateau had been captured by the Germans and was being interrogated, de Blommaert, Boussa and the evaders feared the worst. Could he be relied upon to hold up under torture and not reveal the existence of the camp? 'It is incredible what people say under the compulsion of torture,' wrote the German Jesuit Friedrich von Spee in 1631, 'and how many lies they will tell about themselves and about others.'

The main hope of the evaders was that as the Germans appeared to know nothing of the camps, their interrogation wouldn't touch on the subject. 'The Germans knew a lot of people were hiding in the forest but thought they were all Maquis [Resistance] or Frenchmen trying to keep out of the labour draft,' Captain William M. Davis said and Brayley's diary entry for 18 July reads: 'The Germans remained ignorant that Allied airmen were hidden in the forest, although they were aware that something was going on. They never ventured into the woods to find out. Instead, the patrols contented themselves with machine-gunning the forest paths at intervals. We were continually on the *qui-vive* but no one was wounded.'

It is unclear whether the Germans really did then know that people were in the forest, but the capture of Plateau could change all that if he mentioned the camps under torture. A few days later the camps heard he'd said nothing despite being interrogated and tortured, but he had been sent to a concentration camp. They were safe again, for the time being, thanks to Plateau's bravery.

By the middle of July, both camps had grown significantly. 'There were 120 English, Canadians, Australians, Americans, New Zealanders, Russians and Africans living in our forest camps,' recalled Lieutenant Jonathan Pearson III of the USAAF. 'It was one of the happiest adventures of our lives.' Escapers and evaders continued to be brought to the forest and Fréteval continued to remain undiscovered despite the capture of Plateau and the earlier arrest of Virginia d'Albert Lake.

The sentries placed around the forest edge had proved to be an effective early warning system. 'During the daylight hours we had four guard posts where we would watch in case someone would come too close and discover our camp,' recalled Peloquin. And close by, at the forest lodge where Boussa was staying, the Hallouins were on standby to light a fire as a warning of Germans threatening to enter the forest. 'We spent difficult moments, I prayed to the good Lord very often, but we truly were lucky,' Madame Hallouin reflected.

However, neither she nor the sentries noticed a scruffy figure wandering into the woods one day in July. It wasn't long before he was strolling close to Camp 1, where an alert lookout spotted him and escorted him to Berry. An attempt was made at interrogation, but he couldn't speak a word of English. He obviously wasn't a German spy or a deserter, but little more could be discovered about the man. He didn't appear a threat as long as he remained in the camp, and he was given some of the more undesirable jobs in Camp 1 to occupy his time. It was eventually discovered that he was a Russian soldier from Georgia by the name of Gedfre Chichldse. The Allied evaders gave him the nickname of Cogi. 'Those in Camp 1 would not let him leave for fear he may get stopped and divulge their location,' remembered Peloquin, 'so he became a prisoner among a group of escapees.' William M. Davis had also heard that a Russian had wandered into the forest. 'I think he is harmless and hope he is well treated,' Davis said.

None of the evaders could ever be certain what would happen next but the fear amongst them was that the security of the camps was becoming increasingly at risk. On one occasion Jubault and de Blommaert had been stopped while travelling to the forest by a German patrol. They were questioned and their forged papers examined, but their confident manner and ease under questioning managed to convince the Germans that they were of no interest and they were allowed to go.

To increase the security of the camps the decision was made to move the command post of Boussa, currently in the forest lodge of the Hallouins, to the railway station at Saint Jean-Froidmentel. Just less than ten miles to the north of Fréteval, the station on the Bretigny-Vendôme line was run by station master Demouliere and his wife Jeanne. They belonged to the Resistance and had often lodged evaders before passing them along the escape routes. Despite the fact that the station was still in an area heavily occupied by Germans (right across the railway line they used the château of Rougement as a command post), it was hoped that by moving Boussa here he would be disassociated from the camps should he be discovered. In fact it was an ideal location, the many comings and goings in the station by regular passengers obscuring Boussa's activities.

At his new location Boussa wrote radio messages that his operator, Francois Toussaint, would transmit. Toussaint himself had been moved at regular intervals to avoid detection and was now concealed in a room at the house of Robert Guérineau, the baker at Romilly-sur-Aigre. Communication between Boussa and Toussaint was carried out by Guérineau's daughter, Roberte, who also brought messages from London. Another 'runner' was Pierre Guillaumin. A trusted friend of Jubault, he took over supplying food to the camps following the arrest of Plateau, and established and operated a permanent communication line between Boussa and the camps once Boussa had moved to his new location at the station.

Although he was now located farther from Camp 1, Boussa would continue to make forays there to pass messages on himself. 'He used to transmit messages across to Neave in Oxford Street where the SOE office was, information and so on,' Worrall said, 'and used to come pretty much every day to see us. He told us the Allies had landed in Normandy, and the hope was that they would overrun the forest and get us out. He tried to come every day and if he didn't we got a bit worried. In fact, he didn't come for about two days and we wondered what had happened to him and he then turned up and said, "They got onto my radio operator so we had to keep quiet."'

Boussa and his regular messages to the evaders continuously announced the advances of the Allied troops through Normandy. But there still seemed little sign of the forest being liberated. Boussa's messages consisted of news mixed with rumour and, for the men in the forest, it was impossible to get a clear picture of what was happening beyond the forest boundaries and farther away in France. They were getting impatient. 'We had news every day from London and began to hope for release soon,' Davis explained. 'The men were under great tension and some of them could not wait. We had to guard the camp area and prevent anyone from leaving it.'

Nobody did. They decided to sit and wait. Little did they know that, despite radio reports, the Allied advance towards them wasn't going quite to plan.

CHAPTER 19

THE ADVANCE

Following the D-Day landings of 6 June, the Allies quickly discovered that breaking out from their Normandy beachhead would be extremely tough and fraught with difficulties. The fighting on the beaches had been hard but it was only a taster of what the Allies could expect as they tried to advance inland. The Germans were stubbornly defending wherever they could, realising that there would only be one opportunity to push the Allies back out of France and that would be in Normandy itself. Their defences were helped by the fact that Normandy was a region of woodland and pasture with sunken routes, winding roads and deep, dense hedgerows. It was easier to defend than attack.

While the US forces concentrated on moving west to link the beaches and free Brittany, the British, Canadian and Polish forces (also joined by contingents from the Free French, Belgium, Czechoslovakia, Greece, Norway and the Netherlands) had to capture Caen before they could move inland. The original plan had been for British troops to liberate the city on the evening of 6 June 1944, but the Germans defended themselves against the relentless onslaught. By 14 June, the city was still in German hands and the failure to capture it was causing a serious delay to the Allies, as well as resulting in terrible losses.

Meanwhile, US infantry had reached Carentan and taken the town from the retreating Germans, but a counter-offensive was launched and the Germans had managed to reclaim a position 500 yards from the town. However, tanks of the US 2nd Armoured Division arrived in the afternoon to drive the Germans back once more. Within a couple of days, the 502nd and 506th Parachute Infantry Regiments had established a defensive line and linked up with the men of the US 82nd Airborne Division to make Carentan safe.

The Allied offensive around Caen wasn't proving as successful. It had been hit by bad weather; a storm in the Channel on 23 June prevented crucial resupplies of food, materials and fuel from reaching Normandy. With the Allies unable to advance, the Germans saw their opportunity to reinforce their defences. On 25 June, a new operation, Epsom, was launched to capture the city but by 1 July Caen still hadn't fallen to the Allies, despite it being surrounded to the north and west.

With Caen proving a stumbling block, an American offensive continued towards Cherbourg. A tough fight for the port followed: coastal guns had to be silenced and house-to-house fighting in the narrow streets was ferocious.

Eventually, on 29 June Cherbourg fell to the Allies and 10,000 Germans were captured.

Meanwhile, back in Caen, a controversial carpet-bombing operation followed that softened up the German defences in the city, but it was still left to the Allied infantrymen to take the area with bitter hand-to-hand fighting, the British suffering 25 per cent casualty rates. It was grim, intense and unspeakably violent but, in Operation Bluecoat, the British managed to push the German front line back by 8 miles and seize the high ground to the south of Caen, an area the Germans had previously dominated. In doing so General Montgomery had driven a wedge between General Heinrich Eberbach's Panzer Group West and SS General Paul Hausser's 7th Army. Because of the British and Canadian successes in the Caen area, the Germans had to divert their increasingly depleted forces to the region to stave off the Allied offensive.

Eventually, at the end of July, Caen was liberated. The fierce battle and the fact that the Germans had devoted so many forces to the defence of the area opened up the corridor that allowed General Bradley's army to move out of the Cotentin Peninsula and into central portions of France in Operation Cobra.

By this stage of the war, a faction in the German command had decided that Germany was facing a catastrophic defeat, brought about by Hitler's increasingly irrational management of the war. They decided that Hitler must be assassinated. It wasn't the first time a plan had been hatched to kill the leader of the Third Reich (some reports suggest over forty planned, attempted and failed assassination attempts had been made on Hitler since 1921),[123] but this one would be the closest anyone would come to killing Hitler. One of the integral figures in the plot was Colonel Claus von Stauffenberg, a thirty-six-year-old German officer and member of German nobility.

Operation Valkyrie involved Stauffenberg travelling to the Wolf's Lair, Hitler's top-secret headquarters in Poland, 400 miles east of Berlin. Security was ultra-tight here because Hitler was convinced the Allies would use any means to kill him. He even employed young women to taste all his food to ensure it wasn't poisoned. One of them was twenty-five-year-old Margot Wölk. 'The food was always vegetarian,' she remembered. 'There were constant rumours that the British were out to poison Hitler. He never ate meat. We were given rice, noodles, peppers, peas and cauliflower. Some of the girls started to shed tears as they began eating because they were so afraid. We had to eat it all up. Then we had to wait an hour, and every time we were frightened that we were going to be ill. We used to cry like dogs because we were so glad to have survived.'[124]

Stauffenberg's plan was to attend a military conference within the Wolf's Lair, held in the underground *Führerbunker*. His briefcase, containing two bombs, would be placed under Hitler's table. However, owing to the hot summer weather, the location of the conference was changed at the last minute to a briefing room above ground. It was a major setback for Stauffenberg as the underground bunker was perfectly suited to a bomb causing maximum damage. The blast waves and shrapnel wouldn't penetrate the reinforced thick walls but would bounce back right inside the room, the air pressure generated by the explosion killing everyone instantly.

Nevertheless, Stauffenberg decided to continue with the plot, certain that the two bombs within the briefcase would still cause enough damage to kill Hitler even in the new meeting room. As everyone gathered for the conference, Stauffenberg made his excuses and left the room with his aide-de-camp, Werner von Haeften, to arm the bombs. They went to a private room and began the task but were disturbed by an unexpected knock on the door from a guard urging them to hurry up as the meeting was about to begin. As a result, von Stauffenberg was only able to arm one of the bombs.

He placed the armed briefcase under the table as close to Hitler as possible. There was only person between Stauffenberg and Hitler; it was in the perfect position. Moments later, Stauffenberg excused himself and left the room. But just after he left the room, Colonel Heinz Brandt, in an effort to get a better look at the map laid out on the table, moved the briefcase from where it stood to the other side of a thick, strong table leg. Seven minutes after moving the briefcase the bomb went off, blowing off one of Brandt's legs.

Sitting in another room was food-taster Margot Wölk. 'We were sitting on wooden benches, and suddenly we heard and felt this incredible big bang. We fell off the benches and I heard someone shouting, "Hitler is dead!" But, of course, he wasn't.'[125] The explosion had torn through the room and four people had been killed, but Hilter had been shielded from the blast by the leg of the table and had sustained only minor burns, a burst eardrum and concussion.

Stauffenberg, believing Hitler was dead, left quickly and returned to Berlin but when he heard on the radio that Hitler had survived he realised the coup had failed and retribution would be swift and brutal. Stauffenburg was tracked down and overpowered after a brief shoot-out. He was executed the following day, one of 4,980 executed over the coming months, often on the barest evidence, for being part of the plot. 'I'm sure Stauffenberg was not the right man for the job,' said Philipp von Boeselager sixty years later, one of the team involved in the plot who escaped execution, 'but the truth is he was the only one who had the courage to do it.'[126]

While Hitler was reeling from this episode and extracting his revenge on the plotters, the Allies commenced with Operation Cobra on 25 July, having been delayed several times by bad weather. It began with 1,500 B-17 and B-24 bombers dropping over 3,000 tons of bombs and napalm on enemy positions, putting out of action an estimated 70 per cent of German soldiers (as well as killing over one hundred American servicemen). It highlighted just how important the air campaign was in supporting the troops and hardware on the ground. Lieutenant John Eisenhower, the newly commissioned son of the Supreme Commander of the Allied forces, told his father: 'You would never get away with this if you didn't have air supremacy,' to which Dwight D. Eisenhower replied, 'If I didn't have air supremacy, I wouldn't be here.'

Within two days the 30th Infantry Division reported breaks in the German defences and it wasn't long before 100,000 Allied combat troops had poured through these gaps and established a gateway from Normandy to Brittany. Coutances was taken on 27 July and Avranches three days later as the German defences collapsed. Led by General Patton, the Third Army quickly took most of Brittany and then sped to Argentan. Here the entire German 7th Army was close to being captured. They only had one escape route, through the Falaise Gap, but they were under strict orders from Hitler not to retreat. Within days they were captured, with 50,000 prisoners taken as Patton's tanks headed for Paris.

The Allies were out of Normandy, but they were still a long way from Fréteval where the evaders keenly listened to any news on the radio or messages from Boussa. 'The thing was,' Worrall recalled, 'the Allies weren't landing in Normandy and marching straight through. They advanced a bit, and then they were pushed back, nearly into the sea at one stage. It wasn't just a landing and they came straight through: there was a counter-attack by the Germans. Lucien Boussa used to come and one day he would say, "It shouldn't be too long now before the British get to you," then he would come another day and say, "I'm sorry, they've had to retreat." It was very depressing.'

By the beginning of August, small pockets of resistance were hindering the British progress through France as Panzer divisions counter-attacked, while the American advance was slowed by elements of the German Army, especially in the region of Mortain, which the Americans finally reached on 3 August. As Hitler prepared his 'last chance' operation, Patton reached the German defences at Rennes, 145 miles to the west of Fréteval.

Within the confines of the forest, time was dragging slowly as the August sun bore down on the evaders, the foliage of the trees providing little sanctuary as temperatures rose. Morale within the camps was dropping, the men getting restless knowing liberation was near but with no certainty when it would arrive. And constantly there was the menace of the German troops nearby. 'The hardest thing was the waiting. The radio continuously announced the advances of the Allied troops, but one waited in vain in the region of Fréteval,' recalled Omer Jubault.

The first weekend in August saw the British continue to move slowly forwards, while the Americans were now accelerating in the direction of Le Mans. However, Hitler was determined to counter-attack in the Cotentin region despite General von Kluge, commander of the German force in Normandy, feeling that such an attack would be useless (on 30 July he had written to Hitler warning that the entire Western Front was on the brink of collapse).* Kluge requested permission to fall back towards the Rhine but his request was refused, and German forces assembled with aircraft taken from the Russian front to support them.

---

* General von Kluge had been approached prior to the 20 July assassination attempt on Hitler to use his influence to inspire a mass uprising amongst the troops. Although he refused, his name appeared on a list of suspected conspirators following the failed assassination attempt. On 19 August 1944, fearing Hitler would punish him as a conspirator, von Kluge committed suicide by taking cyanide.

THE ADVANCE

The final major German offensive in Normandy took place overnight on 6/7 August but American fighter-bombers stopped it in its tracks, destroying many of their Tiger tanks while Allied troops begin encircling the enemy. Three days later, the Americans of the 15th Corps had liberated Le Mans, less than fifty miles from Fréteval. For the first time, the evaders within the Camps began to realise that the Allies were closing in. 'At the beginning of August, liberation was no longer in doubt,' recalled Jubault.

As well as hearing the news on the radio and the sound of distant battle, the evaders would creep to the edge of the forest where they could actually see Germans retreating past the forest. 'Nearing mid-August one evening I was posted to lookout duty with a colleague,' remembered Alex Campbell. 'Twilight was approaching when we became aware of a strange commotion approaching from the south-west. Finally, into view came a confusion of men and vehicles in obvious haste. They were heading in an easterly direction and left no doubt they were survivors of an army in desperate retreat.'

'Every night now we could hear the Germans in full retreat,' recalled Murray. 'On several occasions horse-drawn vehicles parked alongside our wood and we hardly dared breathe 'til they had gone by. During the day, Allied fighter-bombers strafed and dive-bombed fleeing convoys and we were careful to camouflage our tents with green branches lest we were also strafed.'

Not every one of the evaders – and by now there was 152 hiding out in the forest – was keen to remain in the forest camps with Germans retreating all about them. They were worried that the Germans would enter the forest as they fled, discover the evaders and massacre them. It was a very real prospect and caused immense tension. Many of the men were eager to break ranks, leave the forest and take their chances out in the open. They knew there were no weapons to defend themselves with although Boussa, anticipating such an outcome, had asked local Resistance groups to create small armed groups to patrol the forest boundary to ward off any German foray into Fréteval.

Boussa was well aware of the feeling of the evaders. They were impatient, desperate and nervous, a volatile mix of emotions that could spur them into making rash decisions that, ultimately, might endanger the lives of everyone in the camps. Somehow, Boussa thought, he had to get the liberation of the camps speeded up. He knew, like the others, that the Americans were 50 miles away in Le Mans. He just needed to get to them. That meant running the gauntlet of the retreating Germans and all that that entailed, but he was convinced that was the only option if the liberation of the camps was to be achieved without bloodshed or massacre.

Boussa enlisted the help of Etienne Viron, the local baker, and the two of them trundled off in the baker's van towards the Americans at Le Mans. Little did he know that when he arrived in Le Mans he would be reunited with the man who had devised this audacious plan and put it into operation from Room 900 in London. And neither of them knew that Operation Sherwood faced one of its most critical moments as the race to liberate the evaders threatened their very safety.

CHAPTER 20

LIBERATION

Neave had been a distant spectator as the D-Day invasion took place and the Allies broke through into France. His only contact with the evaders at Fréteval, ever since the first men entered the camps over two months earlier, had been through intermittent radio communication with Boussa. Neave had known of the near misses, the alarms, the occasional arrests of guides and the disaster of the parachute drops that had affected the safety of the camps. But, incredibly, they had still remained undiscovered by the Germans.

He had estimated that four to five hundred men would ultimately end up in the camps but, as it was, the final number was 152. Nevertheless, it was still a remarkable achievement. Now all he had to do was oversee their safe liberation. This was a task he didn't want to delegate or miss out on. This had been his bold plan, one he had devised, developed and instigated. He wanted to see it through. He wanted to be the first man into the camps and to be the one to liberate the men. He was determined nobody would get in his way.

After Neave persuaded his superior officers that IS9 should be responsible for liberating the evaders at Fréteval, Donald Darling was brought back to Room 900 from Gibraltar, which enabled Neave to sail to Normandy in July 1944. It was the first time he had been back on the Continent since he had escaped from Colditz and, after crossing the Channel, he found himself holed up in Bayeux, 18 miles to the west of Caen. Desperate to reach Fréteval, Neave was frustrated at having to spend almost a month at Bayeux as the Allies fought to break through the Normandy beachhead. He was all too aware of the perilous position the evaders at Fréteval found themselves in.

'My intention, on arrival in Normandy, was to rescue as many lives from the Germans as possible,' he wrote, 'especially of those who now lay at the mercy of the embittered and defeated secret police. From this time until the end of the war, the Gestapo behaved with vindictiveness and purposeless brutality, knowing that Germany had lost the war.'[127] Neave was determined the evaders shouldn't fall victim to them. But, for the time being, there was nothing he could do. The Allies' advance was slow and the pockets of German resistance determined, while the evaders were stuck at Fréteval over one hundred and sixty miles away, still in enemy territory. It would be a long wait for Neave, but an even longer wait for the airmen in the forest.

Neave was anxious about how much longer the men at Fréteval could hold out and he felt personally responsible for their safety. He resolved that as soon as the Allies broke through the Normandy beachhead he would make a dash to the camps. Three weeks of uneventful frustration passed for Neave. He had been assigned a French liaison officer, Capitaine Gilles Lefort, and a Canadian, Major James Thornton, who would help in making plans for the liberation of the camps. Together, the three of them spent July either working on these plans or visiting Caen where, at the front line, they watched the artillery pound the enemy.

When the Americans advanced at the beginning of August and broke through into Brittany, Neave needed no second invitation to load up his jeep and speed towards Rennes, 110 miles south-west of Bayeux. He remembered it as an exhilarating trip as they narrowly avoided ambush, passing through newly liberated villages and along roads that bore the evidence of a German army in retreat, the scattered detritus of battle, corpses, the mangled remains of military hardware, and dead mules and horses lying by the smouldering roadside.

Reaching Rennes, Neave turned to follow the path of Patton's US Third Army that was heading for Paris. It was a route that would take him close to Fréteval and the waiting men. Neave had had sporadic radio contact with de Blommaert during his time in Bayeux, but once he had left Normandy communication had ceased totally as he didn't have any radio links owing to a misunderstanding between the combat area and clandestine operations. But he knew, when he left Normandy, over one hundred and fifty evaders awaited liberation there, and he was determined that he was the man to do it.

Blocked briefly by a German counter-attack, Neave eventually arrived in Le Mans on 10 August. There was a rapturous welcome awaiting him from the local population who had been under German occupation since 1940 and had been liberated just two days before Neave arrived. Consequently, wine was flowing freely. Neave settled into the Hôtel Moderne, a small establishment in the Place de la République and close to the River Sarthe. Despite the celebrations, Neave had other things on his mind. He was desperate to liberate the evaders and his desire to do so increased immeasurably when, talking to an officer of an armoured division in Le Mans, he discovered that the American Third Army, instead of attacking towards Chartres and Vendôme as he had expected were, instead, planning an attack on the Falaise Gap, which would destroy much of the German army west of the Seine. This was a disaster for Neave and his plans to rescue the evaders in the forest.

He had been depending on these tanks and armoured cars to liberate the forest, needing them to help repel the German forces known to be in and around Cloyes, close to Fréteval. Without the support of tanks and armoured cars he only had six jeeps and a few automatic weapons at his disposal. It was nowhere near enough to clear whatever forces were left in the Fréteval area, and even that information was unclear as Neave had had no direct contact with the camps, only intelligence reports that German battle groups had been reported between Le Mans and Châteaudun.

Alarmed, Neave returned to the hotel where he sat in the dining room with Capitaine Lefort and Major Thornton. While excited war correspondents and members of the Free French drank and rejoiced around them, celebrating the liberation of Le Mans, Neave and his two officers poured over a map of the region, desperately planning a route to the forest. 'I was going to be responsible for a terrible tragedy if things went wrong,[128] recalled Neave, well aware that the Germans were panicking as they retreated and knowing that massacres by the SS had been perpetrated against civilians and military personnel.

Eventually, Neave identified a route to the forest but was desperate for transport and armed protection to carry out his rescue mission. Together with Thornton he headed north of Le Mans to persuade the American XV Corps to provide him with some light tanks to carry out the rescue. Pleading his case to a staff officer, Neave was refused both troops and transport. Not only did they refuse to spare the manpower and machinery as they had orders to wait for a move on Alençon, but they considered the rescue operation impossible without light tanks.

Neave and Thornton began their journey back to their hotel. The whole rescue mission seemed in jeopardy and the lives of the evaders potentially in peril. With no communication, Neave was unable to keep them informed of developments – or lack of – and he was certain that the men in Fréteval would be getting twitchy. Neave was depressed; Operation Sherwood had come so far and achieved so much yet now, at the very end, its success was uncertain.

Pulling into the courtyard of the Hôtel Moderne, Neave was greeted by a large number of heavily armed army jeeps with five officers and thirty-four men resting nearby, awaiting orders from London. He noticed they were all wearing maroon berets and discovered they were a British 2SAS Squadron under the command of Captain Anthony Greville-Bell. Later that evening, another twenty-three men, comprising Belgians from 5SAS Squadron, arrived with radios. It was a huge stroke of luck for Neave; even more so for the evaders within the forest, and not before time. They were getting increasingly restless and some had once again broached the idea of making a run for it.

Neave rushed into the hotel lounge and sought out Captain Anthony Greville-Bell. Born in Sydney, Australia, but educated in Tiverton, Devon, he had been awarded the Distinguished Service Order (DSO) for his actions behind enemy lines during Operation Speedwell in Italy in 1943, when he destroyed railway lines, derailed trains and blocked tunnels, despite having sustained broken ribs and damaging his back while parachuting into Castiglione. Having exhausted all his explosives, Greville-Bell and his two companions then undertook a 250-mile march along mountain chains and through German lines to safety. It took them seventy-three days, during which they survived on grapes and tomatoes. The citation of his DSO proclaimed his 'unfailing judgement in the most difficult circumstances and inspiration to those under his command'.[129]

He was just the sort of man Neave needed, and his first impressions of him were of a 'dashing young officer … ideally suited to "private warfare" and no respecter of red tape'.[130] Neave told Greville-Bell about his problem. Listening intently and becoming more fascinated with the prospect of helping out, Greville-Bell left Neave and immediately contacted London to request permission to take part in the operation. The following day he received confirmation that both 2SAS and 5SAS squadrons could help in the liberation of Fréteval. Neave was delighted. Without them any rescue mission would be impossible, but now he finally had what he needed and so, on 11 August, Neave and Greville-Bell along with other officers and members of the Resistance began studying maps once more to determine the best route into the forest.

While they were debating their plan they were interrupted when, out of the blue, Boussa appeared in the hotel lobby. He had left the forest the day before in the baker's van determined to speed up the liberation of the evaders and had managed to track down Neave. Boussa was unaware that after he had left the camp an American jeep with two GIs had pulled up at the forest, having been informed by local villagers of the evaders there. Seeing the airmen, the GIs went off to get them some food and 'later returned loaded up with American food, Spam, coffee and other goodies and we enjoyed the best meal many of us had had for months,' said Worrall.

Despite the appearance of the GIs, there was still the threat of unpredictable, retreating Germans in the area. Worrall added:

The next day we received information that the Gestapo were in nearby Cloyes and that they were on the way to the forest. There was panic and we decided to scatter, but six of us decided to stick together. Others went in small groups to nearby villages where the villagers were astonished to find themselves confronted by people speaking English. The six of us went into a village shop where we were given red wine, and although there was no food there was a girl who could speak a little English.

She went and got some eggs and made omelettes, which we ate washing them down with the red wine. After that, as it was late, we decided to look for somewhere to sleep. We came to yet another village and found yet another shop where we were given yet more eggs and red wine. This time we had an audience of excited French men and women who kept giving us wine and patting us on the back. I think we paid for some of what we consumed because all of us had money from our escape packs on us.

Having drunk to excess a farmer took us to his barn and went to sleep in the hay. In the early hours of the morning we were awakened by the sound of heavy footsteps on the cobbles outside. We all froze, but the footsteps died away to our great relief. We left the farm to return to the camp, thanking the farmer as we did so. As we made our way back to the forest we heard a motorcycle behind us getting closer. Once again, I thought that even at this late stage, 'We are going to get caught and not going to make it after all!' It was a tremendous relief when the rider called out in an American drawl, 'Do any of you bastards speak English?' He told us that an armoured convoy was on its way to the forest.

Almost euphoric, Worrall and his colleagues headed at once back to their camp in the forest.

Although Neave was delighted to see that Boussa was safe and that the men in the forest were still undiscovered and unharmed, he was less enthusiastic to hear that some of the men had already started to escape, venturing to nearby Busloup to see what was happening before returning to the camps to let the rest know that the Germans were in full retreat.

Boussa implored Neave to come and rescue the men immediately, telling him that there were no Germans in the forest and that it was quite safe to come. Neave wasn't quite so convinced that it was as safe as Boussa indicated. He was concerned that the Belgian's excitement had clouded his judgement and didn't want his SAS squadrons to be caught up in a firefight as they approached the forest, especially as he had no clear indication yet which route in was fully safe. Besides, although he'd secured weapons and transport for the SAS, there was no transport to evacuate the evaders from the forest. Neave told Boussa he must return to the camps and tell the men to wait another forty-eight hours until they could be freed, arranging with him a rendezvous point on the edge of the forest. Boussa was devastated but agreed to go back and try to persuade the men to stay put. 'It was a relief when the chief agent [Boussa] from the other camp came to tell us that US units were at Le Mans, and that we would be contacted soon and taken out,' remembered Captain William M. Davis. 'We packed up and waited.'

Neave decided that it would be prudent to send a recce party ahead. Not only would they scout out the area, they would also be able to convince the evaders that they should not disperse and should wait in the camps as agreed. Twenty-three-year-old Captain Peter Baker volunteered to lead the party. However, Neave was wary of Baker, worried that he was more interested in heroism than practical soldiering and was convinced that Baker was intending, as soon as the time was right, to change into civilian clothes and head for Paris to write an article for an American newspaper. Neave knew the seriousness of the Fréteval rescue mission. It was imperative that the unarmed evaders be rescued and not captured, killed or wounded because of one man's impetuousness.

Baker was a curious fellow and Neave had every right to be cautious. The son of an army major, he was described as 'stubby, short-sighted and thoroughly unmilitary in appearance' when he was commissioned into the Royal Artillery in 1940. Transferred to the Intelligence Corps in

August 1942, he joined the mysterious Phantom unit a year later, part of the GHQ Liaison Regiment renowned for its use of brilliance, initiative, cunning and even criminality to achieve its goals. Serving in North Africa and then Italy, Baker was recruited by MI9 to reorganise Resistance groups and escape routes in France and Belgium prior to the D-Day landings. On D-Day itself, Baker crossed into France and helped escaping Allied airmen, POWs and important political refugees get back to Britain before he found himself in Le Mans and volunteering to head to Fréteval.

Eventually Neave agreed to let Baker go ahead to the forest as part of a team consisting of himself and three other men (gunner Mackenzie and two Frenchmen) in their jeep loaded with boxes of rations, two bicycles, Bren guns and Tommy guns, a wireless set and two suitcases. 'It was our task to get to safety hundreds of Allied escapers who were being maintained there by the Resistance, within a quarter of a mile of a German Corps Headquarters,' recalled Baker. 'My first task was to penetrate into the German-occupied territory and contact the Resistance and our agents in the village of St Jean Froidmental. We then had to arrange the evacuation of the escaped prisoners, either back through our own lines or to the South.'[131]

The journey was uneventful to begin with as they drove through countless villages and sped past French peasants and German soldiers who appeared 'undesirous of combat'.[132] In one village they were greeted with such a reception that they were delayed by two hours as they were embraced and toasted by the newly liberated French. Moving on towards Châteaudun, they came across a German soldier emerging from a cottage to collect water. He surrendered and stated he had seven colleagues farther along the road who also wished to surrender. Firing their Bren gun in the direction of these Germans, Baker saw them emerge warily holding a white handkerchief and walking towards the jeep. Baker and his men had just climbed out of their jeep to approach the ragged Germans when a machine-gun in a nearby hedgerow opened up. Rushing back to the jeep the four of them clambered aboard and sped off. One of the Frenchmen had been slightly wounded and when Baker discovered a bullet-hole in the peak of his cap he realised how lucky they had been to escape.

Heading back to Romilly to treat the Frenchman's wounds, Baker found a new route to the forest and they eventually reached Fréteval the next morning when Baker got his first sight of the camps. 'I have never seen so incredible a sight as these men when I arrived with their Resistance friends in a jeep and in uniform. At first, those who saw us were frankly incredulous. Then they suddenly realised what was happening and, calling out all the others, they emerged in a hysterical rush. My companions tried to quieten them but, after the weeks of silence and secrecy and waiting they could contain themselves no longer,' he recalled.[133]

'They had been brought by Lucien,' remembered Berry. 'And they left us saying that the Americans were coming through to let us all out the next day, Saturday, 12 August 1944.'

Meanwhile, back in Le Mans, Neave was still searching

for transport to get the evaders out of the forest. Despite American trucks being lined up in the city, the commanders were unwilling to let Neave borrow them for such a risky venture. The prospect of postponing the rescue loomed once more and Neave was conscious of the effect this would have on the men in the camps. At noon, just as he was about to send another officer to the forest to deliver the bad news, de Blommaert appeared in the city. It was the first time Neave had seen him since he'd taken off from an English airfield in April. De Blommaert told him, 'The men are terribly disappointed that you have not come' and that 'I can assure you that it is safe. This morning several of them have broken away from the camp and are celebrating with the inhabitants of the village of St Jean Froidmental. All the flags are out and the people are bringing their best wine out of the cellars.'[134]

Neave's anger grew, specifically towards the Americans who were refusing to give him vehicles. And although de Blommaert assured him that it was safe, Neave knew that American reports indicated German rear guards were still in the area. Any fight between these rear guards and the SAS would put the evaders at risk. He'd be damned if he'd come hundreds of miles to lose, at the last moment, the very men he came to save.

In the forest, Berry had given each evader 1,000 francs in case they had to escape and buy their own food. By midday, the mood had begun to sink. No one had arrived to rescue them as promised and Berry had heard that the Gestapo were close by in Cloyes. He left the camp to investigate, telling those that remained that if he hadn't returned by 4 pm then something serious had happened to him.

Back in Le Mans, a gloomy, thoughtful Neave had lunch, pondering his actions but determined that the operation should be carried out in one swift movement. Later that afternoon he got a message to go to the main square in the city. He was greeted by the sight of sixteen coaches and trucks, all ready to go and rescue the evaders. A delighted Neave resolved that they would do so the following morning.

Berry had managed to return from Cloyes before the 4 pm deadline. He had not seen any Gestapo in the town, just some Americans being warmly greeted by the locals. While he was away, Berry had missed Boussa who had returned to the camp with news that the evaders would definitely be rescued the next day. Once again spirits soared, although tinged with a touch of apprehension: this wasn't the first time a rescue had been assured.

At 8 am on 14 August, Neave and his collection of vehicles and one hundred troops assembled outside the Hôtel Moderne in Le Mans. 'It was a fine, hot morning and in high spirits we set off along the road to Vendôme with a patrol of SAS ahead of us,' Neave recalled.[135] They travelled as quickly as possible and after forty-five minutes saw the forest. The rendezvous was a clearing by the road and there, waiting, Neave saw de Blommaert, Boussa and a large crowd of men. It was a thrilling moment. The end of a successful operation and Neave could finally breathe easy that his bold plan had worked.

'The airmen were lean, bronzed and dressed in rough

French working clothes,' he remembered. 'Some were angry and impatient. A few had disappeared and ten were taken off by two American tanks on the edge of the forest. I shook hands with Jubault, the gendarme who had done so much to make the plan a success. I could only apologise for our failure to arrive before. Then we turned around and set off at a hot pace back to Le Mans.'[136]

It was not without emotion and perhaps a certain regret that the airmen threw a last glance over their shoulders towards the great forest that had sheltered them for those three long months as they set off with Neave and his convoy. Several members of the Resistance, knowing the evaders were leaving, came to say goodbye.

In total, Neave had rescued 132 of the 152 men in the camp, the others already taken away by Americans or having left of their own accord as liberation neared. They consisted of Americans, Canadians, New Zealanders, Polish, one Russian interloper and, of course the British, including Ray Worrall. 'At the end of the day it was a wonderful experience. It's incredible how I lived through it and got away with it,' he said. 'To have planned and executed a scheme to hide and feed 152 airmen, under the noses of the German Army and the Gestapo, was an outstanding achievement.'

CHAPTER 21

THE END

Just before noon, Neave, the rescue party and the 132 evaders were back in Le Mans. A meal of American rations had been laid on at a former French Army barracks, after which the men washed, shaved and got into new uniforms, a welcome relief having spent months in the same old rags.

That evening, back at Fréteval and alerted by activity in the area, German patrols entered the forest. They found no Allied evader, merely the tents made from tarpaulins, tables and chairs hewn from trees, the makeshift golf course, straw beds and the remains of charcoal fires. Who knows what would have occurred if the Allied evaders had been there when the Germans arrived? As it was, they were enjoying a hot meal and a warm shower in Le Mans, their months of captivity finally over.

Over the coming days the British evaders were transported to Bayeux while the Americans were taken to Laval. They were debriefed by their relevant intelligence agencies before beginning their homeward journey. One sour note was that the lone Russian, 'Cogi', was put in with the German prisoners despite protestations from the British and Americans who had shared the forest with him. 'Cogi', the man who had stumbled into the forest and done most of the dirty and menial jobs for the others without complaint, was never heard of again.

For Neave, it was difficult to believe that Operation Sherwood was over. He recalled looking at de Blommaert and Boussa after the evaders had been rescued and were on their way back to Le Mans and sensed that they could barely comprehend that their extraordinary feat had been achieved 'after three months of suspense'.[137]

It was a remarkable feat of evasion, unsurpassed during World War II. The 152 men had been hidden right under the noses of the Germans. And because most of the evaders were airmen, following their return to Britain nearly all went back into flying operations as the Allies continued to press towards victory. Thirty-eight of the Fréteval evaders were killed in these flying operations or in combat before the end of the war.

Captain Peter Baker returned to Fréteval on 14 August to try to find the ten missing evaders who hadn't been picked up by Neave or the Americans. Arriving at the forest, he discovered they had already been picked up by a passing American convoy but not before he was caught up in a firefight with the Resistance who thought he was part of a German unit. No one was hurt. After this episode, Baker moved on to Chartres to recover more airmen and then on to Paris. On 16 October 1944, while working behind enemy lines in the Netherlands, Baker was captured by the Germans. He managed to escape before being captured again and was about to be shot when a local farmer protested that he didn't want anyone executed on his land. Sent to Stalag XB instead, Baker suffered weeks of brutal interrogation before the camp was liberated on 12 April 1945. Returning to Britain, Baker was awarded the Military Cross in recognition of his gallant and distinguished services in north-west Europe. After the war he became an MP at the age of twenty-eight, but in 1954 suffered a nervous breakdown and had to enter a nursing home to recuperate. His business began to suffer financial problems and the official receiver was called in. His practices were found to be 'suspect' and he was jailed for five years for fraud. His died in 1966 aged just forty-five.

Baron Jean de Blommaert received a DSO for his role in the operation, as well as the French and Belgian Croix de Guerre, and Omer Jubault and members of the Paris organisation were also decorated.

Lucien Boussa received the Military Cross for his actions, as well as the French and Belgian Croix de Guerre. He died on 12 March 1967, just three months before he planned to inaugurate the stone memorial to commemorate Operation Sherwood, which stands on the edge of Fréteval Forest.

The camps at Fréteval weren't the only ones to have sprung up as part of Neave's plans. Operation Marathon was also active in the Ardennes thanks to the efforts of

Albert Ancia. Six smaller camps were set up here with over one hundred men passing through them but Fréteval was, by far, the largest camp and the most impressive feat of evasion. For Neave it was the military exploit of which he was most proud. That 152 men could have lived for three months right under the noses of German forces is almost inexplicable. The evaders did their bit, the Resistance more than did theirs. But it was the plan of just one man, Airey Neave, and it was his effort, his courage and his determination to drive his vision through that made one of the most extraordinary plans of World War II a reality. 'I shall always recall with pleasure our high-spirited journey to Forêt de Fréteval,' he later wrote. 'Viewed as a military operation, it can only be regarded as a calculated risk, but as an exercise in underground war, it was a major success.'[138]

At the time of writing, just one evader remains alive. Ray Worrall is ninety-four years old, but he remembers his adventure in Fréteval as if it were yesterday. He has no doubt about how incredible the whole plan was.

'It's been described as a miracle,' he said. 'I think it probably was.

★

After the liberation of Fréteval, Neave continued through Chartres and was in Paris by the time of liberation on 25 August. From there he went on to the liberation of Brussels on 3 September before serving with distinction in Holland. By the end of the war he had attained the rank of Captain and, in addition to the Military Cross that he had been awarded in 1942, he now held the MBE and the DSO. He served with the International Military Tribunal at the Nuremberg Trials of 1945 and 1946, was awarded the OBE in 1947 and the Bronze Star by the US government a year later. In 1950 he stood for parliament and was elected Conservative MP for Abingdon in 1953.

By this point Neave had 'officially' left his work for the intelligence services, but in reality he never left. Illness in the 1950s held back his political career and when he returned in good health fellow MP Edward Heath told him, 'You're finished.' It was a statement Neave was never to forget. When Heath was challenged as party leader in 1975, Neave threw his weight behind Margaret Thatcher, becoming her campaign manager. She won and offered Neave the chance to shadow any Cabinet post he desired. He chose Northern Ireland at precisely the moment it was replacing the Cold War as the chief preoccupation of military intelligence. It brought him in direct conflict with the IRA, who saw him as 'the architect of a new hard-line British policy on Northern Ireland which would place an increased emphasis on a militarist approach to the political problem'.[139]

On the afternoon of 30 March 1979, Airey Neave, the man who had been the first to escape from Colditz, the brains behind Operation Marathon and Sherwood, and the soldier who had witnessed the liberation of Paris and Brussels, got behind the wheel of his metallic blue Vauxhall in the underground car park of the Houses of Parliament.

Just before 3 pm he started the engine and manoeuvred his way towards the ramp that led up from the House of

Commons car park to central London. Moments later a bomb underneath the car exploded. It was heard across London. Neave, the sole passenger in the car, was rushed to Westminster Hospital, where he died later from his catastrophic injuries. Two groups, the Provisional IRA and the Irish National Liberation Army claimed they carried out the killing. Upon hearing of the atrocity Margaret Thatcher wrote, 'He was one of freedom's warriors. No one knew the great man he was, except those nearest to him. He was staunch, brave, true, strong: but he was very gentle and kind and loyal. It's a rare combination of qualities.'

Airey Neave was sixty-three years old. His life was an epic one, full of courage, determination and the pursuit of the defeat of evil through constant vigilance. Above all he was an unlikely hero, especially to the 152 men who escaped capture, and probably death, by their concealment in the camps at Forêt de Fréteval and who were returned safely to their homes in Britain and other countries as part of Airey Neave's Operation Sherwood, undoubtedly the greatest feat of evasion of World War II.

ACKNOWLEDGEMENTS

We wish to thank everyone who has contributed to the completion of this book. A special thank-you must go to Raymond Worrall, who so freely gave up his time to reflect on his period within Fréteval Forest during World War II, and Roger Stanton MBE, of the Escape Lines Memorial Society, who provided so much help, enthusiasm and encouragement throughout the writing of this book.

Thanks also to Lorraine Vickerman, who helped source information and photographs and who was also a constant source of encouragement and Tashia Munson and Julie Herrada at the University of Michigan, who were invaluable in their help with the US aspect of this story.

Thanks also to everyone at John Blake Publishing, especially James Hodgkinson, who has guided this publication expertly from beginning to end. Finally, a special thanks from Matt to Tom and Rhoda, who have to put up with their dad being immersed in research or writing so frequently and, of course, Lucy for her unwavering support and inspiration and without whom none of this would be possible.

And, finally, Mark wishes to dedicate this book to Alec Langthorne, his father.

SELECT BIBLIOGRAPHY

Arthur, Max, *Forgotten Voices of the Second World War* (Ebury Press, 2007)

Arthur, Max, *Lost Voices of the Royal Air Force* (Hodder Paperbacks, 2005)

Arthur, Max, *There Shall be Wings: The RAF from 1918 to the Present* (Hodder & Stoughton, 1993)

Baker, Captain Peter, *My Testament* (John Calder, 1955)

Barr, Niall, *Yanks and Limeys: Alliance Warfare in the Second World War* (Vintage, 2016)

Barrett Litoff, Judy, Ed., *An American Heroine in the French Resistance* (Fordham University Press, 2006)

Bercuson, David J., & Herwig, Holger H., *One Christmas in Washington: Churchill and Roosevelt Forge the Grand Alliance* (Weidenfeld & Nicolson, 2005)

Bryant-Logan, William, *Air: The Restless Shaper of the World* (W.W. Norton & Co., 2012)

Clutton-Brock, Oliver, *RAF Evaders* (Bounty Books, 2009)

Delarue, Jacques, *Trafics et crimes sous l'Occupation* (Hachette Pluriel Editions, 2013)

Douhet, Giulio, *The Command of the Air* (Coward-McCann, 1942)

Eggers, Reinhold, *Colditz: The German Story* (New English Library, 1972)

Eisner, Peter, *The Freedom Line* (Harper Collins, 2004)

Falconer, Jonathan, *The Bomber Command Handbook 1939-1945* (Sutton Publishing, 1998)

Farmer, Sarah, *Martyred Village* (University of California Press, 2000)

Foot, M.R.D. & Langley, J.M. *MI9, Escape and Evasion 1939–1945* (Bodley Head, 1979)

Garrett, Richard, *Great Escapes of World War II* (Weidenfeld & Nicolson, 1989)

Hutton, Clayton, *Official Secret* (Max Parrish, 1960)

Jackson, Julian, *The Fall of France: The Nazi Invasion of 1940* (Oxford University Press, 2003)

McKinstry, Leo, *Lancaster* (John Murray, 2010)

McKinstry, Leo, *Hurricane: Victor of the Battle of Britain* (John Murray, 2010)

Neave, Airey, *Flames of Calais* (Hodder & Stoughton, 1972)

Neave, Airey, *Little Cyclone* (Hodder & Stoughton, 1954)

Neave, Airey, *Nuremberg* (Hodder & Stoughton, 1978)

Neave, Airey, *Saturday at MI9* (Hodder & Stoughton, 1969)

SELECT BIBLIOGRAPHY

Neave, Airey, *They Have Their Exits* (Hodder & Stoughton, 1953)

Nichol, John & Rennell, Tony, *Home Run* (Viking, 2007)

Olsen, John Andreas, Ed., *A History of Air Warfare* (Potomac Books, 2010)

Preston, Paul, *The Destruction of Guernica* (Harper Press, 2012)

Reid, Pat. R., *The Colditz Story* (Phoenix, 2001)

Routledge, Paul, *Public Servant Secret Agent, The Elusive Life and Violent Death of Airey Neave* (Fourth Estate, 2002)

Sherwood, Robert E., *Roosevelt and Hopkins: An Intimate History* (Harper, 1948)

Spiller, H.J., *Ticket To Freedom* (William Kimber & Co., 1988)

Stourton, Edward, *Cruel Crossing* (Black Swan, 2014)

Vickerman, Lorraine Denise, *My Father's Keepers* (Lorraine Denise Vickerman, 2016)

Watt, George, *The Comet Connection* (University Press of Kentucky, 1990)

Worrall, Raymond, *Escape from France* (Silver Quill Publications, 2004)

Young, Gordon, *In Trust and Treason* (Edward Hulton, 1959)

END NOTES

1 'High Courage on the Axe-Edge of War', Andrew Roberts (*The Times,* March 2007)

2 *The Bomber Command Handbook, 1939–1945* Jonathan Falconer (Sutton Publishing, 2002)

3 *Lancaster: The Second World War's Greatest Bomber,* Leo McKinstry (John Murray, 2010)

4 *Home Run: Escape From Nazi Europe*, John Nicol & Tony Rennell (Viking, 2007)

5 *Great Escapes of World War Two,* Richard Garrett (Weidenfield & Nicolson, 1989)

6 'A Bulletproof Mind', Peter Maass (*New York Times Magazine,* 10 November 2002)

7   *MI9: Escape & Evasion 1939–1945*, M.R.D. Foot & J.M. Langley (Bodley Head, 1979)

8   *Saturday at MI9*, Airey Neave (Hodder & Stoughton, 1969)

9   'Deadly Skies', Robert Fisk (*The Independent*, 2 July 2010)

10 *The Destruction of Guernica*, Paul Preston (HarperPress, 2012)

11 *From Guernica to Hiroshima to Baghdad*, F.C. DeCoste & Bernard Schwartz (University of Alberta, 2000)

12 *The Command of the Air*, Giulio Douhet (Coward-McCann, 1942 trans.)

13 *A History of Air Warfare*, ed. John Andreas Elson (Potomac Books, 2010)

14 *Hurricane: Victor of the Battle of Britain*, Leo McKinstry (John Murray, 2010)

15 'Brave? They Were Scared Witless', Tony Rennell (*Daily Mail*, 17 June 2012)

16 'The Scars of the Second World War Still Line Bomber Country', Neil Tweedie (*Daily Telegraph*, 27 June 2012)

END NOTES

17 'Smoking in the First World War', Chris Wrigley (*History Today*, vol. 64, issue 4, April 2014)

18 *The Nazi War on Cancer*, Robert Proctor (Princeton University Press, 2000)

19 *MI9: Escape & Evasion 1939-45*

20 The National Archives: WO file 208/324, Appendix A.

21 *MI9: Escape & Evasion 1939-45*

22 The National Archives: WO file 165/39, War Diary entry for January 1940

23 *MI9: Escape & Evasion 193-45*

24 Ibid.

25 Ibid.

26 Ibid.

27 *Official Secret* by C. Clayton Hutton (Four Square 1962)

28 During World War II some 2,358,853 of these compasses were produced.

29 'The Escape Artist', Sara Corbett (*New York Times Magazine*, 30 December 2007)

30 *MI9: Escape & Evasion 1939-45*

31 *Home Run: The Escape from Nazi Europe*, John Nichol & Tony Rennell (Viking, 2007)

32 Ibid.

33 'The Escape Artist', Sara Corbett

34 *Saturday at MI9*, Airey Neave

35 *Cruel Crossing*, Edward Stourton (Doubleday, 2013)

36 *Little Cyclone*, Airey Neave (Hodder & Stoughton, 1954)

37 *Public Servant, Secret Agent*, Paul Routledge (Fourth Estate, 2002)

38 *Flames of Calais: A Soldier's Battle 1940*, Airey Neave (Hodder & Stoughton, 1972)

39 *Nuremberg*, Airey Neave (Coronet, 1982)

40 Ibid.

41 *Public Servant, Secret Agent*, Paul Routledge

42 *They Have Their Exits*, Airey Neave (Grafton Books, 1970)

43 'The Postmaster', Merton College magazine, 1990

END NOTES

44 *Public Servant, Secret Agent*, Paul Routledge

45 *They Have Their Exits*, Airey Neave (Grafton Books, 1970)

46 *The Fall of France: The Nazi Invasion of 1940*, Julien Jackson (Oxford University Press, 2003)

47 'The Toast of the French, British Tank Battle Hero Who Stopped Rommel in his Tracks', Robert Hardman (*Daily Mail*, 24 May 2010)

48 *Flames of Calais: A Soldier's Battle, 1940*

49 Ibid.

50 *They Have Their Exits*, Airey Neave (Grafton Books, 1970)

51 Ibid.

52 Ibid.

53 Ibid.

54 Ibid.

55 Ibid.

56 *Public Servant, Secret Agent*, Paul Routledge

57 *They Have Their Exits*, Airey Neave

58 Ibid.

59 *Colditz: The Full Story*, Pat Reid (Macmillan, 1984)

60 *Colditz: The German Story*, Reinhold Eggers (Pan, 1963)

61 *They Have Their Exits*, Airey Neave

62 Ibid.

63 Ibid.

64 Ibid.

65 *Public Servant, Secret Agent*, Paul Routledge

66 *They Have Their Exits*, Airey Neave

67 Ibid.

68 Ibid.

69 *Public Servant, Secret Agent*, Paul Routledge

70 *Saturday at MI9*, Airey Neave

71 'How Dare Channel 4 Defame Airey Neave's Memory', Bruce Anderson (*The Telegraph*, 13 July 2014)

72 *Public Servant, Secret Agent*, Paul Routledge

END NOTES

73 *MI9: Escape & Evasion 1939-45,*

74 Ibid.

75 Ibid.

76 *Saturday at MI9*, Airey Neave

77 Ibid.

78 *Little Cyclone*, Airey Neave

79 *Saturday at MI9*, Airey Neave

80 *Home Run: The Escape from Nazi Europe*, John Nichol
   & Tony Rennell (Viking, 2007)

81 *Saturday at MI9*, Airey Neave

82 Ibid.

83 Ibid.

84 Ibid.

85 Ibid.

86 Ibid.

87 'An Unknown History of the Resistance', L-J Grangé
   (*La Republique de Centre* 10, 12, 17, 19 August 1966)

88 *Saturday at MI9*, Airey Neave

89 *44th Bomb Group Roll of Honour and Casualties* (July 2005)

90 'The Special Relationship Between Great Britain and the United States Began With FDR', David Woolner (The Roosevelt Institute, 22 July 2010)

91 Ibid.

92 *Roosevelt and Hopkins*, Robert E. Sherwood (Enigma Books, 2008)

93 'The Dieppe Raid: The Forgotten D-Day', Gerard Gilbert (*Daily Telegraph*, 17 August 2012)

94 'The Disaster That May Have Saved D-Day', Jason Cumming (NBC News, 6 May 2009)

95 *Air: The Restless Shaper of the World*, William Bryant Logan (W.W. Norton & Co., 2013)

96 *My Father's Keeper,* Lorraine Denise Vickerman (Lorraine Denise Vickerman, 2016)

97 Ibid.

98 Ibid.

99 *Saturday at MI9*, Airey Neave

100 *Martyred Village*, Sarah Farmer (University of California Press, 2000)

END NOTES

101 'Moments of Nazi Massacre Frozen in Time',
Anthony Peregrine (*The Telegraph*, 5 September
2013)

102 *Martyred Village*, Sarah Farmer (University of
California Press, 2000)

103 'An Unsung War Hero Gets Her Due', Laura Griffin
(*St Petersburg Times*, 30 May 1993)

104 *An American Heroine in the French Resistance*, ed. Judy
Barrett Litoff (Fordham University Press, 2006)

105 Ibid.

106 'An Unsung War Hero Gets Her Due', Laura Griffin
(*St Petersburg Times*, 30 May 1993)

107 'A Genuine American Heroine, Jim Calio (*Philip
Morris Magazine*, Nov-Dec, 1989)

108 National Archives & Records Administration,
RG498, Records of Headquarters, European
Theatre of Operations, United States Army (World
War II), MIS-X.

109 'A Genuine American Heroine', Jim Calio (*Philip
Morris Magazine*, Nov-Dec, 1989)

110 'Virginia d'Albert Lake: An American Hero', Judy
Barrett Litoff (*France Today*, June 2009)

111 *Home Run: Escape From Nazi Europe*, John Nichol & Tony Rennell (Viking, 2007)

112 *Saturday at MI9*, Airey Neave (Hodder & Stoughton, 1969)

113 Ibid.

114 *Saturday at MI9*, Airey Neave (Hodder & Stoughton, 1969)

115 'My Father's Keeper,' Lorraine Denise Vickerman (Lorraine Denise Vickerman, 2016)

116 *Home Run: Escape from Nazi Europe,* John Nichol & Tony Rennell (Viking, 2007)

117 *Yanks & Limeys*, Niall Barr (Jonathan Cape, 2015)

118 *Saturday at MI9*, Airey Neave

119 Ibid.

120 Ibid.

121 *RAF Evaders*, Oliver Clutton-Brock (Grub Street Publishing, 2009)

122 *Trafics et Crimes Sous l'Occupation*, Jacques Delarue (Le Livre de Poche, 1971)

END NOTES

123 'Germans Still Split Over Plot to Kill Hitler', Kate Connolly (*The Telegraph*, 19 July 2014)

124 'Hitler's Former Food Taster Reveals the Horrors of the Wolf's Lair', Tony Paterson (*The Independent*, 19 September 2014)

125 Ibid.

126 'Germans Still Split Over Plot to Kill Hitler', Kate Connolly (*The Telegraph*, 19 July 2014)

127 *Saturday at MI9*, Airey Neave

128 Ibid.

129 Obituary of Anthony Greville-Bell (*The Times*, 28 March 2008)

130 *Saturday at MI9*, Airey Neave

131 *My Testament*, Peter Baker (John Calder, 1955)

132 Ibid.

133 Ibid.

134 *Saturday at MI9*, Airey Neave

135 Ibid.

136 Ibid.

137 Ibid.

138 Ibid.

139 'The Airey Neave Files', Paul Vellely (*The Independent*, 22 February 2002)